Collins

need to know?

Triathlon

Joe Beer

"Joe Beer has a knack of making complex science sound simple and a way of translating theory into training in a way that the athlete can easily understand."
Mike Gratton, London Marathon Winner, 1983

"The sport of triathlon has embraced change and experimentation where other sports have been more conservative. Joe has been in the driving seat in the quest for ever greater knowledge."
Graeme Obree, World Pursuit Champion, 1993 & 1995

Collins

First published in 2008 by
Collins, an imprint of
HarperCollins Publishers
77–85 Fulham Palace Road
Hammersmith, London W6 8JB

The Collins website address is:
www.collins.co.uk

Collins is a registered trademark of HarperCollins Publishers Limited
11 10 09 08 07
6 5 4 3 2 1

A catalogue record for this book is available from the British Library.

Created by: **SP Creative Design**
Editor: **Heather Thomas**
Designer: **Rolando Ugolini**
Series design: **Mark Thomson**

Photography
All photography by **Rolando Ugolini** and **Joe Beer** with the exception
of the following:
Adidas: page 25
American Bicycle Group: pages 42–43 and 173
istockphoto.com: page 142 and 143
Mark Lees: pages 114, 120 and 151
Polar: page 46
PowerBar: page 7

ISBN: 978-0-00-726259-5
Printed and bound by **Printing Express Ltd, Hong Kong**

Author's note
As a thank you to the sport I love, 10 per cent of the fee that I received for
writing this book was given to charitable organizations involved in and
outside of triathlon.

Contents

What is triathlon?

Triathlon is a combination of swimming, cycling and running. The competitors perform each sport, one after another, without a break. Changing from one sport to the next, as the clock keeps ticking, is an essential part of an event that embraces different skills and is the ultimate endurance sport. From pool swims to open water, one-hour local events to 17-hour international competitions, triathlon is incredibly varied and has captured the imagination of all age groups, making it one of today's fastest growing sports.

The beginnings

It is claimed that triathlon originated in the United States in the mid-1970s, but there are references to it back in 1920s' France. To do them one after another was seen as the ultimate fitness test and the winner was known as the 'Ironman'. Famously, in Hawaii, in 1978, a group of swimmers, cyclists and runners debated who was the fittest and bet each other that they could not complete a challenge combining the long-established race distances in each sport. Today, there are thousands of triathlons, ranging from short children's events up to the full Ironman distance of a 2.4-mile swim, a 112-mile bike ride and a marathon of 26.2 miles. However, you don't have to be an ultra-fit Ironman to compete in triathlons – you can take part in smaller events that last less than an hour, making it possible to fit triathlon into a busy lifestyle. Many active swimmers, cyclists and runners are, unknowingly, already triathletes, even if they have yet to complete a triathlon.

The benefits

Many triathletes were once single-sport people who were looking for something more exciting and challenging but who still wanted to pursue their initial sport. Varying the sports means that training is never boring, and your muscles are not repeatedly put under loads that cause injury. So don't be scared of taking up this exciting sport – you *can* be a triathlete and you *can* complete a competitive event. Welcome to the exciting world of triathlon.

1 Becoming a triathlete

For the beginner, triathlon can appear daunting, but thousands of people have managed to string together a swim, then a bike ride and, finally, a run to become a triathlete. You can, too. It takes time management, sweat and some specialist equipment, but once you start to think of yourself positively as a triathlete, you can make great leaps forward – everyone has the potential to succeed.

Who can be a triathlete?

Becoming a triathlete is all about thinking of yourself as a jack of three trades rather than a specialist in one sport. You'll probably need to learn a lot about sports that you have never tried before, but in a short time, and with the right level of physical and mental effort and equipment, you can become a triathlete-in-training.

must know

Making the best use of your time in new sports takes time. You need to know many things, such as pool opening times, how long it takes to get changed for biking or the best time of day to go for a run. You will make some mistakes but eventually you'll find what works best for you.

Background and age

Triathletes come from a multitude of backgrounds and age groups. Some realize early in their teens that they want to be a multi-sports athlete, whereas others decide in their fifties or sixties to seek a new challenge. Your reasons for taking up triathlon will be individual to you, and while you may already have some knowledge of one sport, much more will be needed to understand and become proficient in all three sports. That's the crux of triathlon – being competent at three sports at the same time. It's a compromise: frustrating at times but rewarding to those who persevere.

Swimming, cycling and running present us with different challenges, especially as no one skill or piece of equipment transfers over to another sport. Swimming is very skilful and requires regular practice; former child-swimmers will find that they have an advantage here. Cycling is a technological sport in which your equipment can have a major effect on your comfort and speed, but hard work and practice play an important role in creating the perfect synergy of triathlete and machine. Running is simple and low on equipment but it suits lighter athletes and people with little injury history. To blend all three together is an art that makes training constantly varied and fun. Whatever your background, even if it is in ball sports, gym training or occasional fun runs, you can still become a triathlete.

Patience

Wanting to be a triathlete is a worthwhile goal because you can continue competing in single sport events. You will no longer consider yourself as a 'swimmer', 'cyclist' or 'gym rat'; instead, you can think of yourself as a tri-athlete. The important watchword is patience. You cannot translate fitness

Triathletes are jacks of three trades and are of various ages, from pre-teens to pensioners.

must know

Becoming a triathlete is as much a change of mindset as physical training in three sports. You have to believe in yourself and be ready to alter your lifestyle. To ensure you succeed, tell your family and friends what you intend to do and get them on board helping you. It's hard to succeed if you don't have a good supportive backroom team.

from one sport immediately into another. You will not understand all about bikes after one ride, or know exactly what it will take to make you fit enough to complete a triathlon.

If you view this period as a transition, like moving from one sport to another during a race, you will realize that it can't be rushed. Be mindful that you have a lot to learn, you must practise and there are many changes your body must make to morph into a three-sports body type. Enjoy the process and the finish-line feeling will be much sweeter.

There's nothing worse than someone who is so desperate to progress that they take two steps back for each one they try to leap forward. Have patience and the coming months and years of training and racing will be life changing.

The pool is quite likely to be the most intimidating environment for most people who want to become triathletes. Be patient, open to learning and seek out good advice to ensure that you master this challenging discipline.

Pick yourself back up

During the learning process and the new challenges you face, something may go wrong – you may even fail – but don't worry. You just need to be aware that these things can happen and be ready to pick yourself up again and respond in the right way. Maybe work or family commitments interfere with your training or your bike has mechanical problems; these minor setbacks happen to everyone. Feeling tired and as though you are being stretched in all directions is part of everyday life, and you have to squeeze in triathlon training and competition as best you can; it's a case of getting the right balance.

Balancing your training and life is easy with some lateral thinking. You may find it easier and more enjoyable if you go out for a run or a bike with a training partner.

Basic principles

Before you start some serious triathlon training, you need to establish the basic principles and assess your own personal level of fitness as well as your strengths and weaknesses. Here are some general guidelines to get you started.

Start off slowly

Whether you've moved up from one sport to three or have been sedentary up until now, you need to progress slowly with a new sport. Your joints, muscles and tendons will all take time to adjust. Over-strain your body with too much too soon and you may get injured and frustrated. Just because you used to swim, cycle or run proficiently does not mean your body can still do it. Take small steps, not giant leaps. This may mean putting off training with fitter people until you've acquired some basic fitness.

Get sound advice

Your advisers should draw on their experience and be in a position to offer useful training, nutrition and equipment tips based on sound principles. Your ability to filter advice and make it relevant to you is paramount. A good coach can guide you when you have problems and will it make it easier for you to get back on track. Your local triathlon club can advise you on how to go about finding a coach.

Get the right equipment

Triathlon requires more equipment than almost any other sport. You need the correct clothing and tools to train in three sports and eventually compete.

Start with entry-level purchases rather than getting the best or being persuaded to buy something that's a waste of time and money. Apart from what you need to train and compete, less is more. You will have enough equipment to find, sort out and keep maintained without having unnecessary items.

Build your base

It is important to build your foundations in all three sports slowly. This 'base' combines practice in the technical skills of swimming, biking and running with modest-effort endurance training. It gives you the skills to improve your efficiency of movement and the endurance to be able to complete race distances with ease. Having good stamina and skill enables you to add speed later – if needed – without your muscles or co-ordination breaking down.

must know

Your 'base' refers to the accumulation of skills, stamina and strength work that allow you to progress onto speed and competition. Think of it as the base on which you develop specific fitness, and then your performances are on top.

Training with more experienced triathletes is a great way to learn valuable lessons and some useful ideas to help you improve.

Have a goal at all times

Goals don't have to be permanent; instead, see them as tasks to complete, and break down your big targets into smaller, manageable chunks. It may be that your goal is to run twice this week as you did not run at all last week. You also need to get your bike serviced and find out the new pool timetable for laned sessions. Add these together and you've moved forwards. Remember that short-term tasks break down big goals, making them less formidable.

Focus on fun

Training and competing as a triathlete is not about being a 30-hour-a-week hero. Amateur triathletes are normal people who go to work each day and have other things in their lives. Focus on enjoying what you do and dove-tail triathlon into your everyday routine. If your tri-training and competing are in conflict with the rest of your life you may sacrifice the wrong things. Enjoying your sessions and training partners is the reason why we get hooked on triathlon.

Know the seasons

Triathlons occur from late spring through to autumn (April to October in Europe), but training will take place all year round in various weather conditions. You can choose indoor options in winter: e.g. an indoor cycle session instead of training outside in the cold, but embracing the seasons and learning to appreciate crisp winter mornings, running in the rain and warm summer evenings means you are not forever fighting the weather. Be prepared for seasonal changes and have the right equipment.

must know

Daylight stretches to 16 hours in mid-summer but less than eight in mid-winter when training feels harder. Your fitness and motivation will grow as you move through the spring and into the competitive season. There are few medals for being the fittest person on Christmas Day, so relax and have fun with family and friends, but be fit enough to make the most of spring.

Reward yourself

It could be many months before your first triathlon. Meanwhile, you could take part in a single-sport event, such as a 5K running race. It can be a long wait for the tri season to start, so stay motivated by rewarding yourself – perhaps some new equipment when you achieve a training goal. Some people find weight loss easier along the way if a reward is given for each kilo that drops off.

Adapt and grow

You may start with a pool-based sprint triathlon in mind, but later find yourself on the starting line of an Ironman. The sport adapts to your needs, whether you want bigger challenges or just to compete in a few pool-based events. Ironman should not be seen as the final goal for all triathletes – it takes time, effort and sacrifice. See how things develop, and when it stops being fun, try another event or goal.

must know

In the quest to be a good athlete, it's easy to get things out of balance and become too serious. Few people ever make a living from triathlon; it's your hobby. Training sessions can give you space and time to think problems through. It's a highly addictive sport and lots of motivated people converge together – just keep it in perspective.

You won't be short of equipment as a three-sports athlete. Keep it organized and well maintained.

The right environment

If you are going to embark on becoming a triathlete, you have to make sure your environment is right. It's no use planning to take on board new sports if your life is in turmoil and the resources you need are totally lacking. In this case, knowledge is power.

must know

Swim, cycle and run clubs can be useful places to find training partners and learn about non-triathlete events. Many areas now have a triathlon club, which can provide advice, swim sessions and second-hand equipment. For more information, visit www.britishtriathlon.org

Family and friends

Sometimes you may need the support of family and friends – to drive you to an event, pick you up when you have a puncture, or be supportive when you're tired. However, your social network needs to be in balance – if you're going through a family upheaval, it may be better to delay taking on a new challenge. Failure due to lack of support is not the perfect final scenario. If your family can see the positive aspects of your new hobby, they're more likely to support you.

Working lunch

Running at lunchtime or arriving at work by bike is lauded in some quarters but frowned on in others. The support of your boss and co-workers can make a world of difference. Some people have spawned a company tri club or obtained corporate sponsorship. Inclusion in the company newsletter as a fitness hero and role model may boost your promotion chances. At the very least, triathlon is an enjoyable hobby outside of work which is under your control.

Training mates

Triathlon was born out of a desire to be around other like-minded athletes, sharing in each other's misery and jubilation. It's a sociable sport where loners are not the norm – athletes have different goals but they train with others. You may sacrifice your planned training session to help someone, or modify your workouts to train together. It's all about blending socializing, training and motivating one another in a helpful mix. Get a variety of training mates on board; some may be single-sports people you have trained with before or perhaps beginners. Keep their home and mobile numbers and email addresses with you – you never know when you might change a session or be able to hook up with your best buddy.

Having fun with a friend as you train makes the experience of being a triathlete a healthy and rewarding one.

must know

Using a local Ordnance Survey map or one of the online mapping systems, such as Multimap, you can work out smart, safe and manageable routes for training sessions. This can help remove the guesswork and get you back to work or home on time.

Knowing who you are

If you understand your body, your strengths and weaknesses and what makes you tick, you can be more successful. Some introspection will provide useful insight into what will work best for you as well as identifying your potential pitfalls.

must know

Triathletes typically train from five to fifteen hours per week, most averaging around eight to ten hours. You need to devote regular time, but highs and lows are inevitable. Good time management is a skill you'll need to monitor and develop. Keeping a diary can be invaluable for recording which sessions work.

Life so far

Your exercise habits, injuries and past successes are a source of useful information. If you have recurring injuries, your body may need strengthening with specific resistance (weight) training or even require professional sports injury help. Never push an injury that you know will let you down at some point. The advantage of three sports is that you can rest some muscles whilst still staying fit. Your past successes and training habits provide useful clues about your potential and what makes you tick. If you like early morning training but hate exercising after 6pm, heed your preferences and do what you enjoy. With enjoyment comes immediate reward as well as the key to good fitness – consistency.

Assess your fitness

Rate yourself on the following measures (1 low/poor; 5 average; 10 high/good):
- ☐ Natural endurance athleticism
- ☐ Organization of time
- ☐ Resistance to sports injuries
- ☐ Commitment to a plan
- ☐ Managing your body weight
- ☐ Ability to learn a new sport
- ☐ Desire to challenge yourself

How fit are you?

Answering the questions on the previous page will give you an indication of your fitness level. Fitness is transient and you'll lose it if you're inactive for several months. There may be latent fitness below the surface, but it takes time to regain. If you've never done regular sports training, it can get pushed aside by other commitments. However, if you commit to being a triathlete, it will become central to your lifestyle and eventually a natural part of it.

Healthy goals

Being healthy is more than training regularly, getting a personal best (PB) or swimming a mile in less than 30 minutes. If losing weight has always been an elusive goal, make it a parallel one to completing a triathlon, so weight loss is a coincidental benefit rather than the sole reason for training. Conquering past hurdles provides the motivation to succeed. Write down anything that may have prevented you achieving a goal and post this list somewhere prominent to remind yourself of past gremlins.

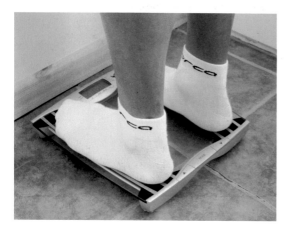

When you need to lose body fat keeping track of your weight means you can gradually move towards the fitter, firmer you.

must know

Make a list of what you need to get before you go food shopping. Base this must-have list on what you've already got at home and what you've run out of. This keeps you on track with your healthy tri diet. You can still have a treat or two but write these down on the list before you head out to shop.

Training is the most significant action you can take to morph yourself into a triathlete. However, your diet is the raw materials for this process.

Diet or disaster

Is your past littered with failed diets, poor eating routines and a lack of knowledge on what to eat? There is so much information on diet, but few people are able to control what they eat, often due to the poor choices on offer. Your training is fuelled by your diet and you are rebuilt from the foods you eat. Quite literally, you are made of what you eat. If poor foods are coming in, the recovery, progress and potential of the human body are massively impaired. Like a formula one engine, you need high-octane fuel if you are to perform well.

Make a list of foods that you have over-consumed or relied upon, then another list of foods that are healthy and you love eating – diet is as much an emotional element as a functional one. Attach the lists to the front of your fridge to remind you to pick the healthy foods and moderate the 'treats'. To become a triathlete you need to eat well, and this aide memoire can help you to develop new healthier eating habits.

Fitness spikes and troughs

If you have been active in one sport and are using this book to move into triathlon, you have a distinct fitness advantage. You already make time to train, probably know how your body works and can reduce your single-sport time commitment as your two new sports provide training variety.

If you have had ups and downs in your fitness and lack consistency, it's vital to find out what causes your enthusiasm to wane to inactivity. Master your inactivity gremlins and you can keep the tri-training going long after previous get-fit campaigns failed.

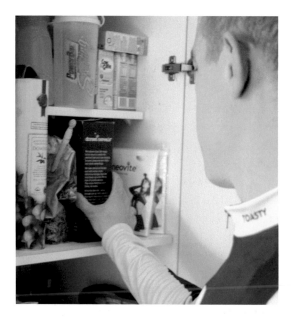

Whatever is in your house is the food that you will tend to rely on. Always buy wisely and enjoy healthy, good-quality foods

Common causes include lacking a goal, doing too much too soon, having unrealistic expectations and impatience. Keep it varied, enjoy your training and you will stay enthusiastic.

Carrot or stick?

You probably have reasons why you do most things but you never really put too much thought into them – if we over-analyzed every action it would paralyse us. So look back and see if your actions have been based on reward (carrot) or possible reprimand (stick). Do you need to be pushed to do something or reined in when you get going due to over-enthusiasm?

Most people have enough commitments, pressures and 'must dos'. What's best for you: to be put under pressure to squeeze triathlon into your routine, or to follow a low-level programme with minimal time

must know

Self-analysis can be quite hard and it's tough to be honest and not kid yourself. Ask a friend to rate your past fitness, your diet and the six questions on page 20. They will probably come up with some useful observations that may not sit comfortably with you but are likely to be fruitful nonetheless.

investment? Some triathletes perform better under pressure but others need time or they will soon drop the sport. You need to work this out for yourself: what mindset are you?

Training preferences

You can train in most weathers if you have the right equipment. It may well be that your summer goal event is cold and wet, due to the vagaries of the weather. If you can train in a gym and not see the light of day all winter, you will have an advantage over triathletes who have to see daylight or get out of the house but need lots of clothing to face the elements. Both mindsets are right: both are training to their preference.

The swim is invariably in an indoor pool all winter, so few people vary their swim training locations. However, bike and run may be indoors or outside which presents varying equipment demands. Similarly, resistance training, pilates or similar exercise classes also take place indoors. If the mood takes you, cross-country races put you in the mud and the wet.

No two athletes will ever have the same experience of what they like best. Write down a 'hate' and a 'love' column on a sheet of paper, recording your past exercise experiences. Think of possible new ones, such as cycling in the rain or swimming in a warm pool, and how they fit into the love-hate designation.

Indoor biking works well when winter darkness or heavy traffic stop morning or evening sessions.

want to know more?

● **To find out more about triathlon, you can check out the website of the sport's governing body, British Triathlon, at www.britishtriathlon.org**
● **For news and events, buy a copy of *220 Triathlon Magazine*, www.220magazine.com**
● **You can find useful articles, race news and results by looking at: www.tri247.com**

Opposite: Varied activities, like AquaJogging, not only give your body a change from running, swimming and biking but also provide something new and refreshing mentally.

2 Goal setting

Before any training, it's wise to have a series
of goals that will direct, motivate and reward
your actions. Rather than have a grand goal
too far away to motivate you and too big
to believe in, you will have to do things in
manageable chunks. Challenging yourself
to do a 'tri' can progress from completing
to conquering and being a real competitor.
Goals are the simple tools you can use to
develop yourself as a triathlete.

Challenging yourself

With no specific event to work towards or a distance to conquer, you are unlikely to succeed in becoming a triathlete. To get motivated, you need a goal that is an actual date in the future. With a challenge comes forth the energy that keeps us positive and fulfilled. Here's your goal-setting homework to get on with.

must know

Triathlons are so popular you often need to enter months in advance. In some cases, they fill up in a matter of hours or days. Even small pool-based events fill up quickly. Be ahead of the game by knowing your goal event(s) and enter as soon as the entry forms are available.

Start with SMART

To make goal setting effective, follow a framework. The acronym SMART provides five criteria to define your goal and ensure you get the most from your training and racing. With this in mind, start refining your goal. Write it down and check the criteria again to make sure they are sound.

Specific

Dreaming that one day you will do a triathlon is not motivating nor likely to become a reality. Pick a specific race on a date, with a measurable distance of swim, bike and run to train towards. Consider recovery time between events, the length of the season (six months) and the early stage in your tri-career. If you've done triathlons before and are taking a refresher course, or have just completed your first season, look back at your best race times. This will give you a useful framework for what is attainable in the future.

Measured

Knowing what you have to complete is an indication of whether your endurance is capable of carrying you through the separate events. If you know you can complete the distance, consider competing against the stopwatch and other athletes. Seeing measured progress brings motivation.

Attainable

Be sure your goal is attainable, taking your current fitness and experience into account. It's unrealistic for an endurance beginner to do an Ironman in one year without physical and mental repercussions. Conversely, a converted time trialist with 15 years of racing might move up to Olympic distance after a handful of sprint events. You can move up distance each season and still be an Ironman in four years.

Rewarding

Know what your ultimate reward will be for doing your triathlon, and consider intermediate rewards to keep your enthusiasm and progress high. Some people treat themselves to a chocolate bar at the end of their biggest mileage week, while others buy a piece of equipment when they complete a race. This approach brings rewards; if the equipment is slowly upgraded, it can help you go faster and make you feel more comfortable about how you look.

Timely

You must have an exact date for your event(s). They do not happen when you are ready to compete but dictate that you must be up to the challenge on a particular square in the calendar. Time may also cause you to adjust the event or the specific way in which you measure success. For example, with good progress, you may move from completion to starting to set goal 'split times' for each segment.

must do

Write down your goals and check them against the SMART criteria. Future life challenges cannot be predicted, so these goals are not set in stone but have to be clearly stated before you can evolve into a competing triathlete.

Having a series of goals makes the training purposeful and more likely to be consistent, especially when it gets hard.

Completing an event

What can seem a huge hurdle to overcome is, in fact, a catalyst to so much more. Crossing your first triathlon finish line not only makes you a triathlete but it also provides an immediate level of merit that few of us can walk away from.

must know

The best estimates are that an athlete takes at least three to five years to be nearing his or her peak conditioning and experience – much more if you are trying to be one of the best of your age group. Like building Rome, you can't become a triathlete in a day.

Make completing your priority

Before we can run we must walk. If you have never completed a triathlon, don't worry – everything is possible. Completing is your priority, so leave competing for prizes for another day. This 'complete-it' attitude does one of two things:

1 In training you have no unrealistic expectations or pressures to beat a certain time. Enjoy training in the knowledge that you can crack the distance but you don't get overly focused on training to a predicted race pace.

2 On race day, enjoy the experience rather than clock-watch the whole time. And, as you have no triathlons to your name and no previous best to beat, it's going to be a personal best (PB) anyway.

Successful transitions

To complete any triathlon you not only need to be capable of the individual distances but also able to 'transition' between the events. This is daunting to a beginner, but with practice and planning it is not to be feared. Triathlon is just a swim, then a bike and then a run. With training and a shorter distance 'sprint' event, you complete the challenge. As long as your first triathlon is one of the shorter distances and you feel it's attainable, completion is possible.

Learning is a long-term process

Even after years of triathlon training and racing, there is still a lot for us to learn as well as many new technological changes to adapt to, so be patient because becoming a fully competent triathlete takes time. Learning about new events and even longer distances takes you through the completion-conquer and compete phases. It takes time to move through each phase – no one can be an expert until they have done something several times. That's the fun that continues to motivate many athletes one, two or even three decades after their first triathlon.

When you get to this point in an event and you have successfully crossed the finishing line, you will know that all the training and hard work has been worthwhile.

Conquering distance or an event

Triathlon is not like a 100-metre race; indeed, it varies so much that no one event is exactly the same as another. Distances may be similar but swim location, bike route demands and run terrain all vary – from pool swims to choppy seas, pan flat to Tour de France terrain, or even cold moors to intense lava fields.

Going 'up distance'

All triathlons are different, so when you've completed an event you want to do more and eventually go 'up distance'. You can do this in one of three ways:

1 Complete a distance a few times, then move up to the next logical distance and format. So, pool-based sprint moves onto Olympic distance with an open-water swim and so on. Thus, taken to its ultimate conclusion, this means you are aiming to complete an Ironman. It's the assumed 'career' path for so many athletes but is not necessarily ideal for all. After completing the 'big one' it may lead to an Ironman focus or a varied future race distance diet.

2 Focus on a distance and conquer the specifics it demands of you. You may then focus on a set distance that suits your time and personal preferences, having tried different event lengths. This career path can spring surprise moves up distance occasionally, but most triathletes have one or two distances they tend to do and they work on improving their course PBs (personal bests). This is probably best for people in the upper third of their age group who may also try to qualify for championships or medals.

3 The give-it-all-a-go option requires you to have a varied diet of events, and tends to focus on completion

rather than ultimate performance, looking for challenges to crack rather than personal bests or age group excellence. This approach suits people who are testing themselves and enjoy the less demanding and often more grass roots events.

Moving up to a greater distance means that some training sessions need to be longer, but you don't have to give up the rest of your life to complete them.

Competing with your peers

Triathlon has children completing short fun events as well as grandmothers competing over Ironman distance for medals. Racing against your age group means that the sport develops as you grow older, so age is no limit to enjoyment and success.

must know

As you get older, your capacity to recover from training will gradually be reduced compared with endurance athletes in their twenties and thirties. New distances can be conquered and personal bests achieved, but you have to train smarter as you get older.

Racing snakes

Typically, the fastest triathletes tend to be in their mid-twenties to early thirties. Once you hit forty, you are considered a veteran (vet) and can compete against your peers in five-year age groups: 40–44,

Triathlon has a multitude of ages and events to challenge you constantly and for many years to come. There are even family events for different ages.

Whatever your age, triathlon is still open to you to compete with yourself, with your peers and with Old Father Time. Many people take up the sport in their forties and fifties, often moving on from single sport disciplines.

45–49, 50–54 and so on. Some very fast vets can win races outright, but most competitors race against their peer group and their personal best rather than aiming to win the whole event by beating fellow triathletes who could be half their age. Although few over-50s can compete with racing snakes in their twenties, they can still be very competitive.

A brave new world

As you get older, a new age group often beckons, giving you plenty of goals. You may find 20 years after your first triathlon that you are returning to events once raced or moving up to a distance that suits your steady but strong constitution. Triathlon started as a challenge, and the events, distances and age groups make it one of the most eclectic sports. This interaction with youngsters who share the same sport may be why older triathletes have a youthfulness that keeps them achieving long after their inactive peers have stopped exercising. This also works in reverse with junior athletes who learn to appreciate and respect the older people they compete against.

want to know more?

● Age group racing makes triathlon suitable for any age. You compete with your peers, and may even get to the Age Group European or World Championship. For more information, look at these websites: www.britistriathlon.org www.ironman.com www.xterra.co.uk

3 Equipment

Triathlon has so much equipment, technology and terminology that it can seem like a totally parallel universe rather than three sports combined. From its inception, challenging ideas and innovation have been central to what makes triathlon, and a triathlete. Rather than spend your money on gimmicks, you need to become equipment savvy. The following pages will give you all the essential information and advice you need.

Swim equipment

The small amount of equipment you need to start swimming should not deceive you into thinking you need only buy a pair of goggles and a swimsuit. Swimming is all about technique, with some tools to improve your skills and others to make you swim faster. You will need the following essential items of equipment.

must know

With all the equipment and plenty of pool time you still need someone to point out what you're doing right and wrong. Bad habits and poor technical ability are the product of swimming alone and never seeing yourself on a video playback. Invest in some swim coaching advice early on, then top it up at regular intervals and you will see progress.

Swimming pool

This is the equipment most triathletes find hardest to manage. Unlike bike and run, which can happen just outside your front door, swimming involves planning and a specific location. Ideally, you need a laned pool, broken into abilities (slow lane, medium lane, etc). Search for a triathlon club session or masters group (see www.britishtriathlon.org for a list of clubs) to give you contact with other triathletes and input from fellow swimmers or a poolside coach. Some triathletes revert to group booking a lane and swimming together to ensure a clear lane and a pleasant session. Whether you pay per session, buy a season ticket or the pool is part of your gym membership, swimming has a cost, and good strokes are the product of hours of training.

Goggles and hat

Secure and comfortable goggles make training more pleasant and help avoid unnecessary injuries caused by swimming into people or objects. A tight-fitting hat means less drag, less wiping your hair out of your eyes and less chlorine damage to your hair. You may get a warmer head but you will have to race in a hat, so see it as race day preparation.

Swim costume

Women wear a one-piece or two-piece costume. Men can have brief-like trunks or a longer cycle-type short. Don't wear baggy costumes or shorts; they make too much drag, forcing you to swim too hard. It's an advanced training method to use a drag suit, so think tight and low-drag when you are buying a costume. Triathlon suits are what many people race in, but the wear and tear, chlorine and stretching caused by regular training will soon make them too expensive to justify training in.

Pool toys

There are three basic tools to help you swim better and learn good technique.

• Fins allow you to concentrate on your arm action and body roll whilst doing a light but incredibly effective foot and leg action.

• A kickboard lets you focus on kicking rhythm.

• A drinks bottle allows you to stay hydrated and provides liquid energy – essential if you are to keep good technique and mental focus from the start to finish of a session.

Advanced training tools

Drag shorts, which are designed to be worn over your normal costume, build strength in swimmers with good technique by adding resistance. However, they are not suitable for beginners, who need good skills before building strength. A set of plastic hand paddles will force you to swim with perfect hand placement or your hands will slip worthlessly through the water; always pick a small pair and then incorporate them a little at a time.

must know

Wetsuits are compulsory in open-water events. They are expensive and you need a perfect fit. They keep you buoyant and warm for maximum progress through the water. Whilst a running vest and swimming costume are adequate, a one- or two-piece trisuit may make you quicker. Get some open water (O/W) goggles with a wider angle of vision and greater suction to the face – useful when the water is cold and dirty.

A good swim pool, with laned sessions, is a valuable resource that so many triathletes struggle to find. Search hard and wide.

Cycle equipment

The longest portion of any triathlon event is the bike leg. This is also the most technologically complicated area of equipment purchase. Money can easily be wasted and expensive equipment can become obsolete if you are not knowledgeable.

Know your bike type

Bicycles come in a huge variety of shapes, sizes and areas of best use. The storage compound for bikes at a race (the transition area) can be filled with mountain bikes, hybrids, racing bikes and specific tri bikes. All allow you to get from T1 (the swim-to-bike transition) to T2 (the bike-to-run transition).

Frame size

When choosing a bike, it is vital to get the right size frame as, unlike many components, such as the three contact points (the handlebars, saddle and pedals), it can't be changed. Sizing your ideal frame size is best done by a bike shop or tri store. You can ask advice and the helpful staff will often pass on some useful tips and tricks, so try to develop a good relationship with them.

The bike frame size that is easiest to measure starts from the centre of the bottom bracket, up the seat tube, to a point where the middle of the top tube intersects – known as centre-to-middle. Manufacturers, mechanics and athletes all vary in how they measure frame size, but, as a ball-park figure, take your inside leg measurement and then multiply by 0.67. For example, 91cm x 0.67 = 60.97 or a 61cm frame.

The exact seat height can be varied by moving the seat post up and down. Similarly, change the distance of the handlebars by changing the stem length. Start with the right frame size and you will be more comfortable, safer and more likely to enjoy your time in the saddle. Correct set up is vital and is well worth the investment in time and money. The bike needs to put you in the right position; don't contort yourself to fit the bike.

As bike speeds are higher than running, heat loss is greater and impacts with the ground harder, so it pays to buy a pair of cycling shorts, a cycle jersey and gloves. Longer or thicker 'longs' are needed if you intend to ride outdoors in winter.

This rider's legs are overstretched. Having the seat too high means that you cannot drop your heel without your hips having to move when the pedal is at its lowest point.

Understanding your bike

Bikes range from the cheap and cheerful types to those costing thousands of pounds. Money spent wisely can allow technology to speed you from the swim-to-bike transition to the bike-to-run transition area as fast as possible. It can also greatly assist comfort and energy conservation. You need to know the basics of a bike to choose the right equipment. Whether it's aerodynamics, bike safety or comfort, you need to know your bike.

Rear cassette
This is a changeable cluster of typically 8, 9 or 10 sprockets that vary in size to provide varying gears. For example, it may have 12, 13, 14, 15, 16, 17, 19, 21, 23 or 25 teeth, called a 12–25 cassette.

Rear derailleur ('rear mech')
This includes a lower and upper jockey wheel that guide the chain to the sprocket selected using the right-hand gear shifter. It will require occasional adjustment to ensure crisp gear changing, minimal noise and no chain derails.

Front derailleur ('front mech')
This guides the chain to one of two or three chain rings using the left-hand gear shifter. Again, it needs to be adjusted correctly to reduce noise and prevent the chain being thrown off.

Chainset
This includes the crank arms the pedals are screwed into and the chain rings that the chain wraps around. Two standard chain rings (e.g. 39 and 53 teeth), a 'compact' version (34/50T) or a 'triple' (30, 42, 52T) give gearing options suitable for any ability and terrain.

Stem

This binds the forks to the handlebars. Some versions allow adjustment of the height and distance of the bar away from the rider. Changing this may prove to be the cheapest way to get more comfort and/or speed.

Handlebars ('bars')

Bars provide a variety of hand positions allowing comfortable seated, out of the saddle and low tuck positions. Either side of the stem is the 'tops', ideal for comfortable training where braking is not needed. Resting on the brake levers, or 'hoods', gives easy selection of gears or braking. Holding the bottom of the bars, or 'drops', with a bent elbow drops you into a fast position with the brakes at hand, ideal for fast descents or into the wind.

Aerodynamic bar ('aero bar' or 'tri bar')

This combination of padded elbow rests and extensions allows the rider to lie flatter, reducing arm strain and increasing speed compared to standard handlebar positions.

Brakes and gear shifters

Brakes are set, as per British Standards, as left operates back brake and right operates front brake. The European set up is the exact opposite but may suit some riders as the right (R) operates the rear gear and brake, whilst the left operates the front mech and front brake. Gear shifting works on a ratchet system that clicks the front or rear gear into a selected gear.

Bottom bracket

This is the axle upon which the chainset rotates. It is the typical starting point for measuring the size of the frame and the rider's saddle height.

Clipless pedals

Running shoes can be used but are neither safe nor comfortable. With a cleat bolted to the bottom of a cycle shoe, these pedals will allow easy entry and exit. Simply press down and you are clipped in; a twist of the ankle and you are clipped out.

Run equipment

Run clothing is as simple as a polyester T-shirt and some shorts. Conversely, running shoes are the piece of equipment that must suit your running style and type of running. They will not last forever, so you need to shop smart.

must know

Running shoes are designed with specific cushioning and stability devices that work when running. Standing around, gardening or cycling in them will damage the cushioning and stability they give you, so use run shoes only for running.

Shopping for your feet

To get the right shoes, you must take your time, try on various pairs and be prepared to walk out empty handed if nothing feels right. Go to a specialist running or triathlon shop, staffed by knowledgeable people. The size of your feet increases in the afternoon, so shop then or take this into account. Wear your normal running socks or purchase some socks at the same time. If you have old run shoes, take them with you as the wear of the underside and cushioning will provide vital clues about what you need. If you have had any serious injuries, accidents or idiosyncracies, now is the time to bring them up – the more the specialist knows about you, the more likely they are to suggest a shoe that will work with your particular running action.

Which shoes are best?

The shoe specialist will look at your feet to assess what type of shoe you need. Many shops now offer a gait analysis service, which can categorize your running style by running over a mat. Some even use treadmills to watch you run and also allow you to test the shoes for comfort.

Never walk away from a shop (or purchase online) with a pair of shoes you have never worn but that are cheap or have been sold on the basis of some miraculous feature. Always try before you buy or your shoes may well injure you and will stop you in your tracks as you train towards your goal of becoming a triathlete.

How many pairs?

Once you know that a shoe works for you, it may be wise to buy a second pair soon afterwards. As models evolve and sometimes disappear, use the internet to search for the shoe that you know works with your feet. Remember also that as new versions appear, older ones drop in price dramatically.

You must be comfortable when running, so try various brands and types until you find what works. When shoes get worn they will increase the chances of injury. Dispose of them before they cause you a problem.

Essential triathlon tools

There are some tools that are essential for successful training and will make it more comfortable, more effective or just more enjoyable. It's not just about swim, bike and run – it's also about training smart with the right tools.

Heart Rate Monitors give you instant feedback on your effort, rate of recovery or pace judgement.

Training diary

From a simple written diary to a high-tech one that sits on your computer, the only way to know what you've achieved so far and what's left to do is to note them down. Seeing sessions you have planned ticked off and the numbers of weeks completed as you work towards your goal is a good indication of the progress you're making. Write down the following information in your training compendium:

• Your training sessions and what you learned about the sport and yourself

• Body statistics, e.g. weight, waist size, and injuries

• Personal bests, e.g. fastest, longest or race results

• Pool times, training partners' telephone numbers, local shop contacts or event dates

• Kit information, e.g. ideal shoe size, bicycle seat height and where/when equipment was brought.

Watch/Heart Rate Monitor

A watch may seem adequate to tell you how long you have been training, but time is not the vital training or racing information you need. A Heart Rate Monitor (HRM) tells you how hard your body is working by sending a signal from a chest strap to a wristwatch. This heart rate value is like a rev counter reading: the harder you go, the higher the number.

An HRM means you have effort (or heart rate) and duration of training (or time) to record in your diary. Many beginners mistakenly believe that an HRM is too hi-tech and too advanced. However, by using a simple test (see page 91) you can know the exact effort to give you most gain with least pain. Harder is not always better, and an HRM is there to tell you honestly what amount of effort you are exerting.

Seasonal conditions

To train all year round, you will need various items of bike and run clothing. One garment will not suit all conditions, so be prepared for an expanding wardrobe. Many triathletes use an indoor cycle trainer to reduce bad weather riding and ride safely when safe cycling facilities are scarce. Riding or running in a gym is also an option that allows sports to be combined and less inclement weather missed.

must know

Triathlon undergoes constant innovation in all three sports. A whole industry has grown out of equipment sales targeted at triathletes. Whereas some items come and go, others are rock solid, so don't waste your hard-earned cash on a pointless toy that is of no benefit.

After you finish a session, your heart rate will drop. If it remains elevated you could be very hot, dehydrated or harboring a cold.

Fads and fallacies

You don't have to spend a fortune on all the latest gear and gadgets. Here are some useful guidelines to making wise purchases and saving money, which will bust many of the myths that have grown up around hi-tech equipment.

Need a tri bike?

You can complete triathlons without needing an expensive tri bike. A good position and an effective training regime beats an expensive bike with a poorly trained rider. However, as your races become longer and you set yourself higher aspirations, you may want to upgrade your bike. Get into the sport on a safe bike you can afford and then wait and see if you want to invest more after your first season.

must know

Equipment that saves you time removes those wasted sessions and kit failures. Well-fitting goggles, quality tyres and inner tubes plus well-kept comfortable running shoes should be your top kit purchases.

A standard road bike is adequate for your first season of triathlon but you may want to move on to a more sophisticated model.

Expensive is always best?

Triathlon equipment purchases, swimming session fees and event entry fees make the sport fairly costly. However, bargains can be had and a great deal of second-hand equipment trickles down to beginners from more experienced triathletes. In all cases, be sure that the equipment is fit for the task, or you will only be buying a different version soon afterwards. Goggles must fit, bike frames must be the right size, and so on. You can save money by ignoring gadgets and fads.

Kit lasts forever?

Nothing will last forever, and some items, such as tyres, run shoes, sports bottles and goggles, require regular renewal. Your equipment must be safe, reliable and assist you in training to your goals. Unfortunately, some triathletes have a 'Did Not Finish' (DNF) next to their name because they use old or badly maintained equipment. With hundreds of hours of training time and much money invested, this is false economy. Wasted sessions caused by punctures, missing kit or even injury due to poor maintenance is a no-brainer.

No need to service your bike?

The bike is your biggest potential headache, so do support your local bike/tri shop by giving them your bike to service once every six months. You will need to discuss what needs replacing and trust their judgement; if in doubt, always get a second opinion. You would not drive a car without a yearly MOT or a service, so make sure you reat your bike with the same respect.

want to know more?

- Check out equipment manufacturers: Adidas (clothing & shoes) www.adidas.com/uk
- Quintana Roo (bikes & wetsuits) and
- Litespeed (bikes) www.americanbicycle group.com
- Snugg (wetsuits) www.snuggwetsuits. co.uk
- New Balance (shoes) www.newbalance.co.uk
- Polar (heart rate monitors) www.polar.fi/polar/ channels/uk
- Tacx (indoor cycle trainers) www.tacx.nl
- PowerBar (nutrition) www.powerbar.com
- Triathlon nutrition specialists www.fueltriathlon.co.uk

4 Your body and your fuel

Good daily eating habits and specific sports nutrition practices can make the most of your general health, fitness improvements and triathlon performances. There are no miracle foods or hard-and-fast rules; personal taste and experience are more important when you are deciding what will work best for your particular needs. You are made from what you eat and drink, so here's how to make yourself fitter and healthier.

Nutrition basics

Becoming a triathlete requires an understanding of not only how nutrition works but also which foods you need to stay healthy, improve your fitness, aid your training and achieve your goals. To train, race and perform your daily tasks, your body uses two types of fuel: fats and carbohydrates.

must know

A varied, healthy diet that includes regular healthy meals and occasional treats and meals out is a good balance that will provide lots of different nutrients and a healthy attitude towards food.

Fats or carbohydrates?

Fat is an abundant fuel, with even the leanest of athletes having over 20,000 calories in their fat stores. This slow-burn, large-capacity fuel allows us to be active for many hours or survive many days without food. The average sedentary person has more fat stored in their body than an active athlete because the former eats more than they need to survive. Excess fat is evidence of previous meals that have been surplus to requirement and stored for periods of famine – an evolutionary mechanism.

When intensity is low to moderate, fat contributes a moderate proportion of the overall calories being used. Conversely, carbohydrates are the first choice of fuel used by muscles for the first 10–20 minutes when starting exercise or working at higher intensities, such as climbing a tough hill or running fast enough to make you breathe heavily. Yet, whilst fat stores can grow indefinitely as a fuel for 'later on', we only have around one-and-a-half to two hours' worth of carbohydrates in our muscles, called glycogen, when we are fully stocked up or 'carbo-loaded'.

Working at high intensities quickly uses this fragile carbohydrate fuel reserve which may require 24–48 hours to be fully restored again. So whilst

you won't run out of fat you can run low on carbs.
Very low glycogen in muscles means slow training,
low morale low and an insatiable appetite.

Knowing you have limited glycogen and teaching
your body to use fats better are key concepts to
understand. They dictate that much of your training
will be steady, but sometimes extra sports nutrition
carbohydrate products should be used to improve
your training and racing.

Protein

Protein from foods such as meat, eggs, milk, fish
and tofu contains the essential building blocks that
are needed to recover and build an athletic body.
You do not have to over-eat protein, as was once
thought, but regular small amounts throughout
the day provide an ideal delivery of building blocks.

**You are what you eat is a
statement that rings true for
triathletes. Ensure you get the
best varied high-quality food
you can to fuel your pastime.**

must know

As you exercise, your calorie burning will increase around 10–15 times higher than if you were just sitting down watching TV. Your appetite will increase and, compared to most sedentary people, you will be regularly hungry and eating often.

Fats

Whilst 'fats' has become a four-letter word in diet circles, 'good' fats are being seen by sports nutrition experts as invaluable to athletes' good health and performance; too little fat in the diet can actually reduce your endurance and can mean constant hunger. Foods that include natural sources of fats, such as olive oil, fish, nuts, seeds and eggs, are ideal for the triathlete to eat regularly. However, reduce any products that list hydrogenated fat in the ingredient list – these are man-made fats that have been linked to ill health.

Vitamins and minerals

These are the widgets that perform many vital functions in the body, such as converting fuels into energy, mopping up waste products and building nervous tissue. Food eaten close to its source in a natural state will be rich in vitamins, but frozen vegetables, well prepared convenience meals and vitamin-enriched foods often contain adequate levels of vitamins.

Many experts now believe that a low-dose daily multi-vitamin that provides 100 per cent of the recommended daily amount is a useful insurance policy to ensure we get the basic level of all the essential nutrients. A diet rich in vegetables, fruits, grains and cereals can ensure high vitamin and mineral intake on a daily basis.

Sports nutrition products

There are many sports supplements that may improve your performance in endurance sports. However, as a beginner your biggest improvement

Farmers' markets are great ways to get fresh fruit and vegetables in season. Find out if there are any regular markets in your area.

will come from working on the skill, stamina and strength aspects of swim, bike and run – there is no magic bullet. Your shopping list is simple:

- The best wholefood diet you can afford
- Occasional treat foods
- A small amount of alcohol if so desired
- A low-dose multi-vitamin and mineral supplement on most days
- Fluid replacement drinks (see page 59).

(see page 59)

A treat, such as a chocolate bar, is not always bad for you. You must eat the majority of your food like an athlete and have treats to keep you human.

Carbohydrate foods eaten to excess merely become fat stores, even if fat intake is very low. Your capacity to process carbohydrates is limited to around 100 grams per feeding, so keep your meals small and regular.

Building aerobic endurance

To become an endurance athlete you have to provide high-quality raw materials in your diet and the right training to allow the body to best adapt. Both good health and good fitness come from feeding and exercising the body in the right proportions.

must know

Less than 25–50 grams of fat is likely to be used in 90 minutes of training if you pace correctly and have a good fitness level. You may use over half your muscle glycogen stores in the same session if the pace is fast or the terrain is hilly. So you always need carbohydrates, even at modest training speeds – whilst fat stores come down very slowly.

Eat fat, burn fat

To maintain optimal fitness, your diet should contain quality sources of fat, amounting to one-quarter or one-third of calories consumed. However, as fat has over twice the energy per gram compared to carbohydrate or protein, you do not need large amounts. A triathlete consuming 3,000 calories in a day needs just 70–90 grams of fat to be in the optimal zone. Research has shown that athletes who cut fat their intake to very low levels actually reduce their fitness and endurance.

High-carb diets

The high-carbohydrate diet, often recommended for athletes and usually recommending that more than 70 per cent of calories should come from carb-rich foods, is actually too high. This leaves little room for fats and protein (only 30 per cent) and restricts food choice. More than 50 per cent is a better target, so you can enjoy carb-rich meals but include good fat and protein sources. Too many carbohydrates in the diet may actually switch the muscles into using carbohydrates instead of fat and cause the body to store fat. Ironically, slightly more fat than was often thought ideal in the diet allows you to be leaner, use fat better as a fuel and eat a more varied diet.

Stress and eating

Aerobic training at a comfortable pace (see page 90) leads to a more controlled appetite and improved ability to cope with stress. This translates into more control of your diet. You binge less, time your foods to suit your activity better and teach your body to use fat as a fuel. Muscles always have to use a small amount of carbohydrate, even at low training speeds.

Losing body fat

To make your body lose fat, you need to create a deficit of calories, i.e. less in and more out. If you exercise an additional 300 calories a day, drop your food intake 200 calories and train correctly you can lose over a pound of weight (450 grams) per week. You are not starving yourself: your body taps into stored fats to cover the deficit and you've made only minor activity and diet alterations. Do this and months later you'll be leaner, fitter and healthier.

The majority of your sessions have to be relaxed cruising. Tag a run after a swim and you get better time management and a transition thrown in.

Hydration

If we are not excessively fat, the most of our total weight is water, which ensures good temperature regulation, waste removal and healthy organ function. As exercise increases, so will your sweat levels and you must know how to be hydration savvy.

must know

Training sessions of less than an hour can be covered using water to wet the mouth and throat whilst cooling the body core. If you notice excessive white salt deposits on your clothes afterwards, you need to drink rehydration fluids and your subsequent meals should contain salt (sodium).

A broken radiator

Your body creates heat as you exercise. Do a spin class indoors or run uphill and you'll soon see sweat flowing from your pores; this is vital to reduce heat build-up in the body. Think of your body as like a radiator that prevents a car from overheating, but only when it is topped up every day. Water is a fragile coolant that we must replace daily. Estimates are around one to two litres of fluids per day, but with varying water content in foods and wide-ranging activity and temperatures, there is no hard and fast rule about how much you need.

In the short term, your body can function with some fluid loss or dehydration, so you needn't carry a bottle on every run. If you let dehydration become more than two to three per cent of body weight or repeatedly dehydrate over several days, problems such as cramping or heat stroke may occur.

Fluid guidelines

Where previous fluid recommendations were for a specific quantity per hour, the latest guidelines suggest using the sensation of thirst as the best way to judge intake. You should not try to teach your body to survive without water in training. Instead, you need to decide when you will drink:

• **Before exercise**: in the two hours before a training session it is good practice to drink 500–750ml water or sports drink to be close to fully hydrated. If you need to urinate in the last hour, water absorption and removal is taking place properly.

• **During exercise**: at the pool, on the bike or out running, a variety of hydration bottles, belts and backpacks make drinking easy – if the session is short, hard work or it's not convenient to drink while training, be sure to rehydrate afterwards.

• **After exercise**: experiment with how much fluid you need after training and what tastes best. If you are very hot, notice your urine colour is very dark and have a dry mouth, rehydration with fluids is your priority before eating food.

You need to think about your hydration throughout the year. If you are thirsty during or after training, then have a drink of water or a sports drink.

Nutrition and troubleshooting

Juggling daily chores and keeping to exact food quotas is nearly impossible. Triathlon training takes up some of your free time and requires you eat the right things at the right time. Here are some common diet scenarios with information on what's wrong with them and how to make them better for your tri lifestyle.

Shift happens

It is self-destructive to be overly critical or inflexible with your diet. Sometimes we do go off the rails, eat the wrong things or plan badly and have to get by on less than ideal food combinations. Being a realist, acknowledging when your diet is wrong and using this to trigger positive action, is most important. Remember that you are human, you are fallible and you will make mistakes.

A bowl of cereal with milk makes a quick and easy high-carb meal that can be a great recovery snack after training sessions at any time of the day.

Case history: **Nick**

Nick trains first thing in the morning, running for 45 minutes, but it always feels like hard work and uncomfortable. He often finds it difficult trying to plan meal timing and quality, but all is not lost.

Meal	Problem	Solution
Breakfast Cereal and milk Slice of toast spread with marmite	Uncomfortable to do a morning run after food. Fat use plummets due to high blood sugar. Digestion poor.	Run before breakfast for a more comfortable run and improved training. A hot drink to wake you up before running is OK but always eat breakfast after training. Benefits: • Better at fat burning • More enjoyable session
High-fat lunch Bacon roll Crisps and chocolate bar	Lots of bad fats will flood the system and are likely to cause drowsiness. Feeling bad about the poor-quality meal will conflict with trying to be a healthy triathlete.	Acknowledge it as a slip-up but don't beat yourself up about it. Instead, make a healthy evening meal to immediately take control of what you eat. • Acknowledge treats as OK • Take control of your diet
Late supper Due to socializing, supper is cobbled together from anything that's left in the fridge	Alcohol can impair your judgement of food quality and quantity. Late eating and alcohol cause poor quality sleep & recovery for Nick regularly. There is a greater chance of fat storage with late-night fatty meals combined with alcohol.	Late night eating does happen, so ensure that you can make as light and healthy a meal as possible. There is no need to be teetotal, but plan late sessions when you can lie in the next day and don't indulge in too many late nights.

must know

Up to 60 minutes after exercising, a golden window of opportunity is open, allowing carbohydrates back into tired muscles. Eat higher carb snacks at this time and you will recover faster and will not over-indulge later.

So little time

The benefits of adding training into your small free slots before work, at lunchtime or as part of your commute cannot be underestimated. You get to do your session and still have more time later on in the day. This training-first approach means that you fit in your swims, bikes and runs but food can be an afterthought – or can even be missed out totally. Sometimes exercise replaces a meal, often as part of excessive weight loss or in those athletes with psychological food issues. If this is the case with you, it requires professional intervention, starting with a visit to your GP to talk the problem through.

Why not cycle to the shops to do your food shopping? Just take a rucksack or some panniers and you can combine your training with a necessary chore.

Case history: **Bill**

Bill tended to put training at the top of his priorities and, with a busy job, he often missed meals or grabbed whatever food was near to hand. However, some simple planning, lightening up about trying to be perfect and treating his diet as central to being fit could him make progress faster as a triathlete.

Meal	Problem	Solution
No breakfast Training in the pool before work leaves little time to eat before being at work by 9am	By 10am blood glucose is very low, so chocolate or a bun is tempting – the first food of the day. This will only be a short-term solution as blood sugar demands are greater than one treat can supply.	Take some squash or a sports drink to the pool. Immediately afterwards, eat a banana sandwich.
No lunch A run crammed into the lunch hour with no time to eat a meal.	Poor recovery from run as well as being at the mercy of hunger and the mid-afternoon munchies. A quick-fix snack will be grabbed at some point with dubious nutritional value.	Reduce run time and have a pre-prepared tuna salad. This may have to sustain you to 5pm and, in some cases, until your evening training. A 4pm mini snack is ideal if you want to train soon after work. You could also talk to your boss about taking a longer lunch hour and finishing work 15 minutes later.
Simple supper Convenience meal with a side salad and small glass of red wine.	Ready-made meals can be good or bad in their nutrient quality. The glass of wine, however, makes you feel guilty and serves to undermine your productive training day.	Choose wisely and these convenience foods can form part of a healthy, balanced diet. It's vital to aim for balance and not perfection.

Case history: **Frances**

Checking what foods you have, what you need and making an exact shopping list means you come back from the supermarket, deli or corner shop with the right choices. Frances always got confused and this led to training and fitness problems.

Meal	Problem	Solution
Breakfast Cornflakes and milk with orange juice	The very fast release of processed foods causes blood sugar to spike, then drop fast, causing a need for snacks by 9 or 10 am. You may also feel constipated.	A slower-release food with more fibre can make you feel full for longer. Try high-fibre cereals with chopped fruit. Herbal, green or fruit tea can help the bowels move early in the day.
Big lunch Over-indulging at lunch in an 'all you can eat' buffet whilst on a course	Excess food makes you feel too tired to train at a normal evening session. You feel bad about not being able to control your eating.	The odd feast is good for recovery but you must stop before gluttony kicks in and you eat because it's there. Eating a healthy breakfast stops you being too hungry and overeating to compensate.
No supper Still full from lunch and not having trained, Frances does not think she needs supper. She succumbs to a reheated half of pizza later on	You still need a little food even if you've had a big lunch. Leave it too long and you'll binge to catch up on missed calories. Don't eat just because you've trained; even on rest days or when you're ill, you still require food.	If you miss training and ate too much lunch, a healthy supper restores the nutrient balance. Eat foods you enjoy which are nutritionally sound. A healthy salad would be ideal with some fruit – high in nutrients, fibre and moisture. Good to help bowel movement early the next day.

Writing a shopping list in advance makes it more likely you will buy healthy foods and avoid the ones you don't really need.

Healthy need not be hell

You can enjoy your diet, have some treats and also experiment with new and exciting food and drink varieties. Regular training in swim, bike and run ensures that you can better manage your weight. However, there are a few people who will still gain weight or never lose the fat they want to shed. The solution is to see food quality and quantity as the best way to build a fitter, stronger more healthy you. Incorporating healthy options or new foods into your daily diet means getting a greater variety of nutrients and moving away from the foods that were not working for you.

As always, especially if you have a very busy schedule juggling your work, family and training commitments, try to plan your meals in advance. You will find that food shopping is much easier and quicker if you have a list saved on your computer ready to print out when needed, or you order direct from the supermarket online – they will deliver direct to your home. Alternatively, make shopping part of your training programme and run or bike.

want to know more?

• For more information on sports nutrition and a healthy diet for athletes, seek out the following books: *Complete Guide to Sports Nutrition*, **Anita Bean (A & C Black)** *Sports Nutrition*, **Jeukendrup & Gleeson (Human Kinetics Group)** *Sports Nutrition for Endurance Athletes*, **Monique Ryan (Velo Press)**
• You will also find useful articles in tri specialist magazines

5   The skills

Being a three-sport athlete entails learning three different sets of skills. You cannot become a good swimmer just by running or a good biker by spending more time in the pool. There are some basic principles to get your triathlon training off to a good start. Alternatively, they can be viewed as useful refreshers for the experienced triathlete to go back and practise regularly.

Skill school: swim

Swimming is more about technique than working hard; you must be smooth, save your energy and relax in the water. Practising good technique makes swimming progressively easier. However, it's a skill that most people will lose quickly, so you need to be consistent and enjoy and make the most of your pool time.

Your head

Where you look acutely affects the rest of your body. Look somewhere between straight down to the pool bottom and 45 degrees ahead. Your neck flexibility and torso position will affect what feels best. Do not bend your head too far under, as turning the head to breathe becomes very difficult. A good rule of thumb is that the water line should hit the forehead area of your swim hat. When breathing, your lowermost eye socket should always stay in the water.

Good technique

For every movement you make there's an appropriate reaction elsewhere in your body. Lift your head out of the water to breathe and your legs drop. Swing your arms too wide and your legs move outwards in the opposite direction. Because water is so dense, if your action is to try to force your way through you will only expend a disproportionate amount of energy. Remember that it is good technique, not brute force, that leads to effective swimming. As Taoists say: take the line of least resistance.

Your arms

The majority of triathlon swimming propulsion comes from your arms. However, you can greatly reduce drag and glide further each time you push off the wall by outstretching your arms, one hand on top of the other, with your head tucked in-between. It may not add propulsion but it makes you better at maximizing the fastest part of your swim – the push off from the wall.

Your body

You need to be flat in the water, not with your legs dragging or your head high out of the water. The more water you displace, the more energy you need to expend and the greater the drag on your body. Your body type and shape may affect how you lie in the water. Body changes in terms of fat, muscle and overall weight can change body position. Using fins, a pull buoy, kick board or a wetsuit can teach correct body position (see page 76).

Breathing

You have to be able to breathe relaxed in order to stay aerobic, maintain the right body position and feel confident in the water. You must exhale under water in such a way that your head rotates sideways and your mouth lifts clear of the water to breathe in. By breathing out, you remove carbon dioxide build-up and this keeps your body relaxed. Holding your breath will only force carbon dioxide levels up, making you breathe in a stressful manner.

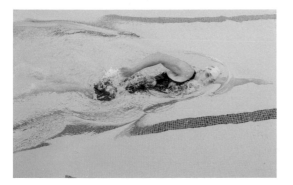

Your legs

Your legs act to balance the stroke, much like a rudder, and provide some propulsion forwards and upwards – they steer, propel and lift. The action should be initiated from the hips and include some knee bend as well. Feet need to be relaxed, not pointing towards the pool bottom. The action should be rhythmic with minimal spreading apart sideways of the feet.

Stroke basics

Swimming is a very difficult skill to learn, especially as it forces breathing to be more conscious and synchronized. You need to get your stroke basics practised, practised and practised again. It takes time and focused learning of each component of correct propulsion, breathing and timing.

Entry

From the high elbow with relaxed hand recovery (see page 69), the flat hand enters the water just ahead of the head and in front of the shoulder. The hand goes into the water, downwards with the forearm and elbow following through the same hole created by the hand. This results in a rolling over on to the side of the body.
• Wrong: outstretched with a flat forearm splash, reaching across your forward-looking eyeline or swimming with no body roll.

Stroke elements

Swimming well is not all about how many metres you cover but what you do in those metres. Understanding what each part of the stroke is trying to achieve means that you know if you are getting it right or wrong. You cannot think about it too much as this results in paralysis by analysis. However, just focus on yourself and stay relaxed.

Catch

The palm must be turned back to face you, whilst still keeping the elbow high in the water. The hand is drawn backwards, pulling you past that point in the pool. The hand is looking to maintain pressure on the water and not slip.

• Wrong: pulling inwards to the other side of the body or letting the elbow drop early in the catch.

Pull/press

Continue with this pulling backwards of the hand just below or alongside the body. This continues until the hand is alongside the thigh, elbow still slightly bent and palm facing backwards. Some experts suggest twisting the palm inwards at this stage before recovery. The arm should accelerate through this phase from the initial slower catch stage. The opposing arm extends as the propulsive arm finishes off, causing a body roll.
• Wrong: pulling under the other side of the body, overextending the arm at the end of the press or failing to speed up the arm action through this phase.

Recovery

From the end of the press, the arm has released pressure on the water and the elbow lifts the hand out of the water. The hand remains low, just above the waterline, as the elbow lifts forwards. The hand is relaxed with either the palm backwards or facing you. The hand then passes the head and is set up for a flat palm entry.

Breathing

To get adequate oxygen, most swimmers breathe every second or third stroke. Breathe out slowly soon after your head returns to its neutral position after breathing in. As the opposing arm enters the water and the shoulder/torso rotates, lift your head, so the water line is just below your mouth. Your mouth opens and you will immediately inspire (breathe in) with little need for you to take a heavy in-breath.

• Wrong: trying to both expire and inspire with your head out of the water, holding your breath too long or lifting your head too high to breathe.

Kick

As the metronome of the whole swim action, the kick needs to be rhythmical. Aim to initiate from the hip with the knee slightly bent on the downward action. On the upward lift, the leg is straighter. Do not try to over-emphasise your kick; it should not be as propulsive as your arm action – remember that a triathlete also has to bike, then run. Eighty to ninety per cent of the event is yet to be completed when you exit the water.

Drills and tests

To focus on each phase of the swim action, specific drills have been designed to help you. These allow you to break the stroke down into its separate components and do each one properly. Some tests of your swimming ability are useful for checking on your progress and knowing what you need to focus upon.

Doggie paddle

This is a short catch-press paddle movement of the arm from outstretched in front to finishing in-line with the shoulder. It is key to keep the elbow high in the water. Recovery is under the water by pushing the hand straight out in front. The head is lifted up to allow breathing, and a normal kick is used, although this is deeper due to the high head position.
• Benefit: this allows the catch (see page 71) to be learned without breathing rushing the process and encourages a high elbow during the catch.

Pettits

Lying flat in the water, place your arms at various positions of the pull and press phases (see page 72). At each point, leave the arms still but move the hands to feel the pressure of the water for 10 sculling movements before moving to the next part of the stroke. You will need to lift your head up between efforts to get a breath. Leg action is very light to ensure hand/forearm propulsion is felt fully.
• Benefit: a feel for the water at various phases of the propulsive phase, especially when you are completing the full stroke.

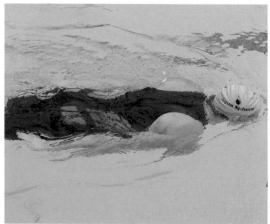

Single arm

Swim with one arm only and the passive arm outstretched in front. Breathe in a relaxed way and continue with your light leg action. Stroke competency is easy to pick up when you are using just one arm at a time.
• Benefit: tests relative left and right arm strength and skills.

Catchup

With both arms outstretched, one arm begins the catch whilst the other stays outstretched. The stroke is completed by the active arm until it extends alongside the passive arm, both shoulder width apart. The passive arm then starts a complete stroke cycle and the previously active arm stays passive. The kick must not be exaggerated to keep the swimmer from sinking; it is about timing and effective propulsion.
• Benefit: this drill emphasizes propulsion and rolling of the body.

Shake offs

Swim with a normal action but pause the hand as it passes the head in the recovery phase. With a relaxed wrist and loose fingers, flick the hand, then continue with a normal entry. This is often easier to do properly using fins to provide propulsion.
• Benefit: teaches a relaxed recovery arm and good body position.

Speed test

Swim 50, 100, 200 or 400m against the clock as fast as you can. Don't totally let the stroke fall past as you will swim slower and you will actually be practising poor rather than good technique.

• Benefit: this drill gives you the opportunity to swim fast and see if you can get a PB.

Kick-only

With a kickboard in your outstretched arms, shoulder width apart, focus on kicking only. Keep the hips, knees and ankles relaxed but effective in propulsion. Good for warming up, breaking up upper-body focused swimming or when your legs are tight from running.

• Benefit: improved kick action and reduced oxygen use by the legs.

Push test (above)

From a push off, with no kicking, see how far you can glide and how your body position affects your streamlining ability. Four to five metres is a good distance and means you are 20 per cent down the pool with no strokes.

• Benefit: focus on using the push off to save strokes.

Stroke count (right)

Over 100m, count your total number of strokes per length; you may need a helper to count for you. This gives you an idea of your efficiency. Good swimmers are 14–18 strokes; over 25 per 25m is a lot of wasted energy.

• Benefit: you can see if drills are making you more efficient.

Skill school: bike

The bicycle is a mere 150 years old and you could even be the first person in your family tree to ever ride one. You will need balance, co-ordination and road awareness to be safe and effective on two wheels. Let's take a look at the basics of biking.

must know

Riding on grass when practising balancing, dismounting or even signalling can make any falls considerably softer. Choose flat grass with little debris or obstacles.

A relaxed riding position will keep 60 per cent of your weight on the saddle and the remaining 40 per cent on the handlebars.

Bike basics

• You will need to use a helmet in all road sessions. With correct sizing, they are comfortable, well ventilated and useful if your head hits the ground.
• Wearing bright clothing, using an LED rear light in low light and always riding as prescribed by the Highway Code will help you to stay safe and upright.
• Although indoor riding is a necessity for many triathletes, races are outside on tarmac, with wind, other road users and the usual ups and downs. You must be able to ride outdoors, so a safe riding position is essential. If you don't sit right on a bike that is correctly proportioned, you will be unstable and unsafe.
• To allow good balance, the saddle should be flat. Use a spirit level to check this, taking into account that any padding can distend under load.
• To be a confident cyclist, your brakes should be easy to reach and work properly.
• Tyres also affect handling in a big way and thus they need to be inflated to around 100–120 psi, depending on the brand and model.

Correct saddle position
Three rules of thumb for correct saddle position are:
1 The seat height should allow you to rest the heel

of your shoe on the pedal at its lowest point while your leg should be fully straight. If your hips have to roll excessively to allow this, then you are too high.

2 The horizontal distance between the front of the saddle and bottom bracket should be around 3–7cm (1–3in). Use a plumb line dropped from the nose of the saddle. You should not have the front of the saddle closer to the handlebars than the bottom bracket – this will be unstable and poor at climbing.

3 The distance between the front of your saddle and handlebars should be the length of your forearm and outstretched fingers plus 5–7cm (2–3in). Further than this and you will be over-reaching.

Your forearm length to the finger tips should be 5-7.5cm (2-3in) short of the handlebars.

A plumb line from the centre of the knee will fall through the rear to front of the pedal, depending on rider preference.

must know

Practising your bike skills is as important as building your fitness. Like a pilot, you will need to log many hours before you can feel fully confident to control your machine. Ride your bike often and enjoy learning to become a cyclist.

The rear cassette comprises eight to ten sprockets, which are selected using the handlebar gear changers.

Pedal action

Your legs need to apply most pressure during the downward phase of pedalling. With clipless pedals, you produce a small amount of upward lifting at the back of the stroke, but this is not the crux of cycling power or efficiency. Choosing the right gear to suit your effort level and the terrain will come with experience. Spin too fast and your legs will move little more than the air around them. However, push too hard a gear and your knees take a lot of strain plus you will tire easily.

Gears on most triathlon bikes are 12-25 on the rear cassette and 39/53 or 30/40/52 on the front chain rings. The larger the rear sprocket size, the easier the gear becomes. On the front chain rings the 'big ring' has you travel further per revolution, so small front-big rear is an easy gear for steep hills. Conversely, a big front-small rear combination gives you a large gear for downhill or tail-wind situations. Vary your gears to find out what feels best and what is clearly the wrong gear - if possible, ride with more experienced riders and watch and listen to their gear choices and changing patterns.

Cadence

The number of revolutions your feet rotate per minute is called your cadence. The optimal number is around 80-100, depending on your muscle size, the terrain and what gear you choose. Riding with more experienced riders lets you see their cadence and helps set a rhythm that you can follow. A cycle computer showing cadence will help you focus on your pedal action - this is better than speed, which can be very slow uphill despite a high effort.

At this point in the pedal action or soon afterwards, you are exerting close to the maximum pressure. Focus on a smooth pressing action that pushes the pedals firmly as the other leg recovers on the upward stroke.

Always be aware of your pedal position as you corner. The inner pedal can scrape the ground and throw you off the bike.

Cornering

In the real world you have to be able to corner safely and without wasting energy. If you slow too much, you have to reaccelerate; brake too hard and you can skid off. On sharp corners, get your inner pedal up and press the outer foot into the pedal at its lowest point. Looking where you want to go and lowering your body makes directing the bike easier. On slight bends, you may be able to pedal through them. Choose a course with a series of twisting descents and junctions to practise cornering.

Skill school: run

Running is the simplest of the three triathlon sports, but it is plagued by injury and a host of overly-complicated phrases and technologies. The keys to successful running are developing a good personal style, wearing the right shoes and avoiding injury.

Avoiding injury

Running is very injury prone, so always keep an eye on how often and how far you run; only increase your distances in small amounts and never run if you are injured. You can still keep fit by going to the pool and doing some AquaJogging (see left) and using out-of-the-saddle riding on hills to build up the muscles that are useful for your running. Above all, take care not to get injured in the first place.

There is no secret to being injury free or running fast. You have to be low weight (within your personal highs and lows) and have regular run training under your belt – there are no aerodynamic aids, just consistent running. It is the last sport in your multisports event, so fatigue will be at its highest.

Your ability to run efficiently, even when tired, is vital to your getting to the finish line. Wanting faster times means you must learn, over time, to be able to run hard in spite of many bodily signals telling you to slow down. For the first season, completion is the key, even with a fading style.

Running style

Of the three sports, running is the one that is most likely to show your personal style. No two running styles look exactly the same and you should run in the way that feels most comfortable to you, not impose someone else's style on your own. Your mechanics of movement are the result of your limb lengths, muscle attachments, flexibility and muscle development – or lack of them.

If you have a previous injury history, try to ascertain the cause: training mileage, hard surfaces, worn shoes, running tired, being overweight or running too hard too often. Injuries stop people training, finishing events or even being able to run again. Be honest with yourself and you may find a weakness that can become a strength.

Urban running is high impact due to tarmac and concrete. Mix this with running on grass, footpaths and mixed surfaces to vary impact levels and provide different cambers.

must know

Running is the most injury prone of the three sports. Make sure that you do not run with worn-out shoes, tired legs or an injury. If in doubt, swap your run for a swim or cycle.

Head and shoulders

When you're running, keep looking forward with your shoulders relaxed, not hunched. Looking down at your feet will restrict your breathing and make your shoulders tense. Only look down if obstacles require that you focus more on exactly where your feet land, as on a rough, stony path. On more even, flat surfaces, just let your feet land where it feels natural and think about relaxed breathing.

Running relaxed is the key to being able to run off the bike. Practise running relaxed in your training and it will convert to relaxed race performances.

Arms

These balance your body in distance running, providing a metronome for your legs to work to. Poor arm technique (as in a fatigued triathlon run) only serves to make the legs feel sluggish and unresponsive. Gently cup your hands and move your arms, like your legs, in the way that feels most natural to you. They will most likely cross towards the middle of your torso.

Body

Your torso should be vertical or slightly leaning forward. Bending too far forwards forces downward head tilt; slumping at the waist restricts breathing. Run tall, with your body erect, not slumped over.

Legs

Your stride length should mirror your effort and the terrain – shorter and higher knees on uphills; longer and faster leg turnover on slight downhills. On the flat, run at a relaxed tempo. However, if your goal is fast running, your legs must move faster but do not over-stride – think fast feet, not big strides.

Feet

On flat terrain, your personal style means that each foot could land heel, mid foot or forefoot first. Uphill, it will be forefoot only (with a strong arm action), whereas downhill the foot 'strike' could be heel, possibly midfoot. This determines which shoes you need, so seek expert advice, possibly by being watched running on a treadmill, to know what style of strike you have and which shoes work best for your biomechanics.

want to know more?

• To learn more about developing your triathlon skills, take a look at the following specialist books:
Triathlon Training, Dave Scott (Simon & Schuster)
Total Triathlete, Allen & Babbitt (Contemporary Books)
Running over Forty, Bruce Tulloh (Tulloh Books)

6 Training

Training is the key process that transforms
a want-to-be person into a capable triathlete.
There are no short cuts and no get-fit-quick
schemes – there is no substitute for your time
and work. But how many times should you
train per day, per week, per month? Should
you swim, go for a run or get on your bike?
In this important section, the ideas behind
training are explained, making this a chapter
to read and return to in the future.

Starting off

It is important that you view your preparation for a session and the way you start it as vital steps to success. You must be organized and plan your sessions carefully. The first triathlete out of the door and up to race speed does not win.

must know

Every session must have a warm up but this does not equate to wasted time or get excluded from the total workout time. As well as being aerobic, warm ups can bridge the gap between normal daily life and the core of your workouts.

Cerebral training

Before doing any stroke, revolution or stride, you need to decide what you are trying to achieve in the session. You can do this as you change into your kit. If you just want to chill after a really bad day at the office, that's fine. If it's a day for working harder, then get yourself mentally ready. To train smart, you must have a goal, some kind of a plan and sessions that fit within both of these parameters.

Leave enough time or adapt

If you lose time and have only got 45 minutes to fit in a session that normally takes an hour, you must adapt your session plan. You may find some days, such as weekends, are better than others for longer sessions. Time management is the skill that good triathletes master. If you are bad at apportioning your time, consider how you can be more efficient with the 10,000 minutes available each week.

Warming up

You have an idea of what you need to do, and you have enough time to do it. However, the dangerous part is approaching: you are about to be let loose. Here is an important piece of advice: you must warm up gradually in the first few minutes of your

leisure time workout fix. Far too often, due to insufficient time, lack of patience or the need to keep up with training partners, triathletes start off too hard. This places physical and chemical stress on their body which leads to lack of progress, injury and burn-out. Some easy relaxed swimming, cycling over flat terrain in low gears or a walk-jog-run is how every session must start.

All three triathlon sports require you to warm up by taking it easy for 10 minutes before starting harder or more technical work.

All systems go?

Given that you spend the first 10–15 minutes gradually increasing your effort from the slowest possible pace up to a steady effort, you can check how your body feels. It might ache a bit, you may feel sluggish, the weather might be horrible, but if there's something that's really serious, such as an injury hurting or an illness in your system, you should stop and end the session right there.

Aerobic base training

Triathlons are aerobic endurance events and may last for hours. Training consists of extended periods of swim, bike and run to teach the body the priority big 'S' (stamina). Learning about the aerobic energy system and how to train it is very important.

Aerobic versus anaerobic

Steady-paced exercise that lasts several minutes or many hours, using oxygen to convert fats and carbohydrates into movement, is aerobic, i.e. with oxygen. Conversely, very fast efforts, e.g. 100-metre sprint races, can be achieved with no breathing, and are pure anaerobic efforts, i.e. without oxygen. If you go at the highest sustainable pace for one or several minutes, you will be using both aerobic and anaerobic energy systems. This produces a burning sensation and extremely heavy breathing.

'Base' or 'endurance' sessions are done at a 'guilt producingly easy' pace, so the muscles, blood, heart and lungs become more efficient at using fats. They may get harder as muscles fatigue, but they are fun and provide time to chill while thinking about good technique. These sessions should make up at least 80 per cent of your weekly training time.

Heart rate monitors

A heart rate monitor (HRM) can be used to assess your effort in bike and run sessions. There are three simple exercises that you can do:

1 During bike or run sessions when you are nose breathing (see 'must know', left), check what heart rate you see just before you have to revert to mouth

breathing. This gives 75–80 per cent of maximum heart rate, or the upper limit of aerobic training.

2 When you are racing or giving a sustained fast effort, see what heart rate you can maintain. When your breathing becomes erratic and the burning sensation in your muscles is overpowering, you have just gone past your anaerobic threshold. This will be around 80–85 per cent of maximum heart rate, or your short distance racing pace.

3 This exercise is optional, as it requires you to push yourself to the limit. It's best done on a bike indoors where few accidents can happen. Gradually increase your speed by 1mph every 2 minutes until you are flat out, then try to sprint for 30 seconds. A helper should see your HR (heart rate) peak in this sprint effort. This is your maximum heart rate, or the peak value if you failed to push yourself to exhaustion. Running max HR will be around 5–10 beats higher.

If you feel how hard you are working and refer to a heart rate monitor (HRM), you can keep your effort at the right intensity.

Throwing 50m of strides into a base run makes it fun, varied and breaks up the time.

Building the base

Depending on your goal and training history, the length of your endurance sessions can vary. A runner turned triathlete can do a long run that a novice to endurance sports could not safely complete without fear of injury. Personalizing your sessions to your circumstances is vital to progress and injury prevention.

Specific stamina

Your bread and butter is endurance training – not weight training, back-to-back interval sessions or core stability sessions. You need to swim, bike and then run for around one hour minimum – up to 12 or more hours if you get the bug and enter an Ironman event. Your muscles need to learn to be efficient and cope with extended periods of effort.

The so-called sprint distance triathlon (750m, 20k, 5k) is wrongly named as even the best athletes take 50–60 minutes. Know your goal distance, and over several months you can build up slowly to be able to do 100–150 per cent of race distance. This prevents a need for sudden jumps in training, and you feel in control of what you're doing. If you have never done endurance training, even 10 minutes' running is a strain on your body, while a 30-minute bike ride feels like a lifetime. So, despite the long sessions talked about by other athletes, start small.

Increments

Build up slowly rather than assuming that in every session or every week you must make progress. Any running mileage increases – both the longest and the total per week – should be very cautious.

Swimming can place strains on the shoulders, especially if poor technique is combined with big hikes in swim volume. Cycling is easier on the body and coasting allows respites that swim and run do not possess. You can 'float' your legs around without actively pressing the pedals. Getting used to pressure and comfort in the feet, backside and hands is the most important feedback as to how far you can ride. Once this is mastered, one hour can become two with a small amount of extra drinking or eating.

Less is more

Not only beginners but also experienced athletes, rarely do swim, bike and run sessions each day. If extending your endurance one day in, say, running, the next day recover by focusing on technique at the pool. Don't get hung up on hitting a set number of hours per week. If you're tired, take an easy or rest day; if you feel good, you can train productively.

Base training converts to better race endurance and speed. It makes it all worthwhile when you go faster than ever before.

Body cycles

Women are aware that their body follows a monthly cycle. Wake up, men! You also have a cycle, which, if correctly manipulated, means both sexes can train, absorb and progress better with forward planning. It's not stargazing but a simple formula for effective adaptation, putting recovery right up there with training.

must know

If you are irritable or feel tired during training sessions and the fun of training has become a compulsion, it's time to have some easy days or maybe two back-to-back no-training days. Rest or recovery will normally do the trick.

Building and recovering

Even though you train regularly every week, it may not necessarily mean that you are building ever-longer sessions. However, the day-to-day training can build up to a level of overload until you recover. This will not happen if you just take a day off – recovery may actually take many days, especially if your training has been to a new level.

If over-reaching, i.e. training without recovery, persists, you will get tired and most likely injured. At the very least, you will go stale. So the simple but effective formula is three weeks training, then one week recovery. That makes a month, so you can work with your body cycles or, at least, impose one.

Work backwards

Smart people will work back from their goal event: at the end of the fourth (taper) week of a cycle (see pages 118–119). This allows you to train by imposing which weeks you will feel good and ensuring from the very start of your triathlon training that the fourth week of recovery is as important as the three training weeks. Note that when you are training for Half or Full Ironman events, a two to three week taper is usually used.

Dovetailing

Every training programme is stress plus recovery, and the classic three-week build and one-week recovery may not work for everyone. It may be sooner than three weeks in older athletes or those who are less resilient and always seem to break down physically. If this is the case, a two-week build and one-week recovery scenario may be worth a try. It may not fit into the perfect monthly cycle, but few things are ever perfect in life.

If you work shifts, have regular trips away or times every month when your work is manic, a pattern may be imposed on you. The key is to use the times when you know that training is less likely for recovery and not to fight whatever is in your way.

Recovery is vital to rebuilding your body after hard training sessions or big weeks. Sleep and naps are the best remedy.

Strength endurance

The fastest triathletes are not bodybuilders but expert three-sport exponents. Building strength can be achieved in the gym, but eventually it needs to be translated into swim, bike and run. Strength is important, so do you need to juggle your gym time?

must know

Each sport imposes some resistance, but it's how you manipulate it that is key to successful training. Biking with a large rain jacket may make more resistance but it can also cause over-heating and ineffective sweat loss. Similarly, running with an excessively heavy backpack can injure the athlete and result in far more loss of training than gains in strength.

Resistance training

Whether you need to add weight training (resistance training) to your plan depends on your reasons and priorities. It may be for rehab, cross-training and health or just for personal aesthetics. However, people who spend lots of time in the gym, such as strong weight trainers and body builders, cannot often swim 750m or run 5km. Their bikes may also creak under their excess muscle mass which is not necessary to complete a triathlon.

You may need to develop greater speed once you have completed events and wish to compete. However, this often does not require greater muscle mass but merely better coordinated muscles that have had suitable base training and the right mixture of resistance and anaerobic work.

Swimming

Water is 1,000 times denser than air and a very hard medium in which to go fast. Even the best swimmers only just creep over 4mph when swimming a mile. The rest of us are most likely to swim at 1–2 mph, possibly 3mph. Even using two swimsuits or drag shorts quickly makes for specific resistance training. You get to make the water feel harder work before peeling off and then swimming faster.

Cycling

On a bike, the opposing forces providing resistance can be hills, wind or rear-wheel resistance from an indoor trainer. On an easy day, pick flatter outdoor routes and use easier gears. Fast cyclists are strong and can spin big gears when hills approach. To get stronger, climb inclines in a gear one or two teeth harder than normal; if you climb in 39 x 21 normally, do it in 39 x 19 at a lower cadence to impose resistance. For many starting out, hills themselves will present enough resistance. Don't work too hard too often – remember the 80:20 rule (see box right).

Running

This imposes varying resistance with hills, treadmill incline, steps or pool running. Moving your weight uphill makes any rise in altitude require more effort than flat running. Shorter efforts can emphasize good form, e.g. 10 x 50m uphill with a jog recovery back down. Rolling terrain or long hills can produce strength through repeated effort against gravity.

Riding in bigger gears can both improve your strength and make your pedal action smoother.

must know

In order to improve at the optimum level, 80 per cent of your weekly training time should be easy to moderate effort. The remaining 20 per cent can be at moderate to high intensity. You don't have to work hard if you don't wish to; 100 per cent easy to steady training effort will still get great results.

Tips and tricks

Finding a programme to fit their lifestyle is the biggest challenge facing budding triathletes. Self-coaching requires you not only to have a plan but also to be able to change it as circumstances alter. Here are some tips for moving up the learning curve.

must know

By trying out various training times and sessions you'll find what slots work best for you. Always let other people, such as your family, workmates and friends, know where you are and when you'll be likely to return

Shift happens

It's easy to have a plan but find that it's hard to have the time or energy for training. Using one of the plans in this book (see Chapter 7) will be a starting mould which you still have to hand-craft to suit your needs. No one plan fits all and no plan fits you all the time. When time is at a premium, pick off the sessions that work on your weaknesses or the sport(s) that need most focus – be flexible.

Technique works

It's not a waste of time to do an easy effort session to focus on your technique – work on your sloppy right arm in the pool or practise corners and gear changing on the bike. If you don't know when to change gear as a hill approaches or what your swim stroke should look like, then your technique session could be watching or being with more skilled athletes. Training is about being smart – using your time and energy wisely. Technique or skills days allow recovery from longer or harder efforts.

Ask an expert

Many times, when things go wrong or you have various options on races, equipment or training groups to choose from, you would be wise to get a

second opinion. Weighing up any choice in life is easier if you consult a second brain, ideally with a few years more experience in the sport to feed off. So before making important decisions about your training regime or target events, ask around and get some expert advice. You make the final judgement yourself, but let others guide you.

This swimmer is performing a one-arm drill to improve his technique. Technique is the first part of being good at any sport.

Transitions

Transitions are the fourth discipline, taking you from swim finish to bike and from bike to run. They vary in their length, degree of crowdedness and the obstacles they pose. Think about transitions as they are the key to saving energy for the real racing.

must know

Being a triathlete is about not just one fast element or 'split'; it's also about the complete package. Having a fast swim split is pointless if you have disasters in T1 and T2 plus you walk half the run. You have to think, train and race with everything from start whistle to finish line in mind.

Welcome to T1...

As you reach the poolside or the edge of a river, lake or the sea, the swim has ended and T1 begins. You may just have to remove your hat and goggles and jog out of the pool to your nearby racked bike, but it could involve half a mile of running in your wetsuit, climbing steps and trying to miss literally hundreds of other athletes. Know what your planned event's T1 is like and build it into your training. A useful skill is to swim 200–1,000m, then haul yourself out of the pool, or every 100m in a 800m swim before walking to the far end of the pool, jump back in and carry on. Some events necessitate you get out halfway, duck under lane ropes or run up the beach and dive back in.

No two transitions are the same from the end of the swim to the start of the bike. The key is to know where you are on the transition racking. You have to don the appropriate clothing, put your helmet on, and only then can you pick your bike up. You wheel it to the mount line and you're off on the cycle leg – the clock does not stop.

... and T2

As you finish the cycle leg, there will be a dismount line. From there onward, you are on foot in T2 until you are out on the run. This involves wheeling the bike to your transition racking point and then removing your helmet. Those athletes using cycle shoes must change, whilst those cycling in run shoes are ready to go. As you exit T2 and start the run, the hard part of triathlon hits home: you still have cycling legs and they are not yet ready to run.

This bike-to-run transition, known as a 'brick', is worth practising many times over, e.g. 6 minutes bike plus 4 minutes run repeated 3–6 times. It can be done outdoors or using gym equipment. An ideal session is when you're on the road; gym training can get boring. The more you practise, the better your muscles get at making the transition and your brain becomes at dealing with heavy legs trying to run.

Learn to move between the sports smoothly and study the layout of every race transition area in minute detail.

Flexibility

It may not be clear exactly how much we can actually alter our flexibility, and it does appear to be genetic. However, repeated training can make our muscles tight or prone to injury, so how much flexibility does a triathlete need?

must know

Your flexibility potential and level of muscle development are both genetically determined. However, your flexibility and muscle size can be developed; the former in easy relaxing processes, and the latter by very hard resistance training. As a triathlete you will need flexibility, not super-sized muscles.

What do you need to do?

Each sport dictates you move your body in a certain pattern of movement. You don't need to be as flexible as a gymnast but poor flexibility makes you move inefficiently, wasting energy and slowing yourself down. Worse still, tight muscles may initiate a vicious cycle, leading to more tightness and so on. Watch a fast athlete: their muscles may be working hard but they are fluid and without compromise.

As a multisports person, you need your muscles to be supple and able to adapt to differing demands. For example, poor shoulder flexibility could affect your swim stroke, especially the recovery action. Similarly, poor lower back flexibility or an injury can make a tucked cycle position hard to hold. Running is the hardest sport on the body and many people run with tight hamstrings, poor hip flexibility or upper body tightness. None of this makes for a fluid runner, especially after a swim and bike.

Improving flexibility

There are several ways in which you can assess and improve your flexibility. Try the following:
1 Get a sports massage, which includes flexibility exercises. The practitioner should be advised that you are a triathlete and they can then seek out

muscles that need massage and flexibility work.

2 Soon after training, stretch lightly, holding your muscles for 30 seconds, without pain, and having been shown the correct stretch. Research suggests this may help to maximize your flexibility potential.

3 Relaxing after training or in the evening by doing some light limbering exercises is great for relaxation and muscle recovery. You should perform short stretches of about 6–10 seconds duration within a comfortable range of movement.

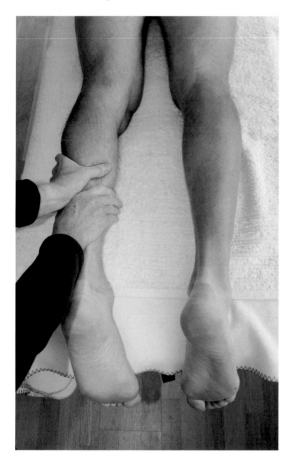

Making good use of empty time can mean you keep your muscles supple, but do be careful never to over-stretch them.

Getting a massage is a great way to treat yourself and have a once-over that can prevent injury and improve recovery.

Anaerobic training

Building the aerobic base can produce good health, solid fitness and the capability to complete endurance events. However, if you want to go even faster, you need to add the top-end anaerobic training. Here are some basic guidelines to how to achieve this.

must know

Recovering from some high-intensity training requires days of lighter training, so focus on good nutrition and ensuring that you get a good night's sleep for several nights. If the opportunity arises for snatching a catnap of 20-30 minutes in the middle of the day, take it; it will help all aspects of your life.

Why do anaerobic training?

High-intensity efforts (speed work or interval training) take you above the 80 per cent of maximum point to a place where effort begins to focus the mind. At this point, your body shifts over to exclusively using carbohydrate for fuel – you stop burning fat. The by-product lactate (lactic acid) makes movement awkward, breathing laboured and muscles burn. This potent training can, in small doses, add a few more per cent to your top speed. However, the bulk of your fitness still comes from the base you build. Intervals are not a get-quick route to higher fitness.

Speed work

Triathlon may be an endurance event but once you can complete the distance, i.e. you have the stamina, the next element to think about is speed. This high-intensity training is the icing on the aerobic base you build with your steady endurance sessions and technique work. Examples of speed work are:

- Swim: 10 x 100m at 2 sec/100m faster than race pace with 60 sec recovery
- Bike: 7 x 3 min at 90 per cent HR with a 1 min spin between
- Run: 7 min at 83 per cent, 7 min at 85 per cent and 7 min at 89 per cent HR back-to-back.

Doing harder training in pairs or groups brings out the extra effort you need to make it effective.

In each case, the hard work only amounts to around 20 minutes, but it is very potent and does not need to be constantly added to. Less is more; if you follow these guidelines, you will feel strong, come away from the session before you fatigue and get faster.

The warning label

The downside of anaerobic training is that it causes stress to the body and can, at times of high stress elsewhere in your life, just make you tired, not fitter. Only do it when your body is ready for it. For most beginners, this means a total focus on base training for six to eight months before adding small amounts of speed work or racing. Don't rush into speed work; concentrate on building good technique and a solid aerobic base first. Always have a good aerobic warm up of 10-20 minutes before high-intensity work.

want to know more?

● For more specialist information, look at the following books:
Triathlon Training in Four Hours a Week: From Beginner to Finish Line in Just Six Weeks, Eric Harr (Rodale Books)
Swimming (Triathlon Training), Steve Tarpinian (A & C Black)
Breakthrough Triathlon Training: How to Balance Your Busy Life, Avoid Burn Out and Achieve Triathlon Peak Performance, Brad Kearns (McGraw-Hill Contemporary)

7 Training plans

Triathlon requires you to balance three sports, each with its own technical and physical demands, and having a training plan can take the guesswork out of what to do. It can also ensure that you get the important sessions completed when your time is short. You are different to all other athletes in your genetics and lifestyle, but everyone needs a plan.

How to use the schedules

At the very least, you need a plan to give you an idea of how to train and what proportions to train in each sport. Good technique and endurance are your priority before building more speed and competence. If you fail to plan, you are planning to fail.

must know

Training requires that you find what works best for you while tweaking things to suit your personal situation, fitness level and goals. Keep a log of what you do and you will learn a lot about which sessions were successful and which were mistakes.

Seasons

In the UK and most of the northern hemisphere, triathlons are held from April until early October. Most triathletes compete from May to September, so after a seasonal chill out of two to four weeks the winter training starts in October or November. This structure gives a logic to your yearly schedule.

In the winter, you can build your endurance ('base') and technique. This is followed by spring progressive training which blends into early races and season-specific sessions. Some training is clearly not about goals but getting out of the house, burning off stress and seeing your friends. However, most sessions allow you to get better because they are targeted at a specific triathlon weakness.

Build and recover

The plans in this chapter suggest sessions, but you decide if you have recovered from your previous training or need to reduce or delay training for a day or so. To progress, you must build sessions that overload you more than before, although eventually you'll have to recover. Don't do several long or hard sessions back to back. Similarly, each fourth week reduce the quantity and frequency of your training. Don't try to do more; it's time to recover and just catch up on your work commitments, chores and the like while you have some extra spare time.

New ideas, small doses

These plans are not the only training you should ever try but they are an effective starting point. If you do want to integrate other ideas or sessions, be very clear on one thing: you must add any new sessions only in small doses to see how they affect you. Change too many things at once and you will not know which factor creates what effect. Above all, keep your training simple and fun.

You need to plan ahead, train and then review what happened in order to learn and progress.

Beginners

Beginners with no background in endurance sports must start slowly and just enjoy what is a total change of lifestyle. Begin by committing to just three or four training sessions a week; this is a big change, so don't try to get ahead of yourself too quickly.

Keep the effort easy

This training plan will be enough of a change from your usual routine without doing it too hard too soon, which can result in injury, extreme fatigue or mental staleness. It's early days, so just enjoy your new lifestyle as a triathlete.

	Week 1	Week 2	Week 3	Week 4
Mon	Swim 15–20 mins. Single lengths with rest between. Keep count of total.	Swim 25 mins. Single lengths with rest between. Keep count of total.	Swim 25–30 mins. Single lengths with occasional double-lengths. Keep count of total.	Swim 15–20 mins. Single lengths with rest between. Keep count of total.
Tues	Rest	Rest	Rest	Rest
Wed	Run 10–15 mins. Alternate walk 1-min, run 1-min.	Run 15–20 mins. Alternate walk 1-min, run 1-min.	Run 20–25 mins. Alternate walk 1-min, run 2-mins.	Run 15 mins. Alternate walk 1-min, run 1-min.
Thurs	Rest	Rest	Rest	Rest
Fri	Rest	Rest	Rest	Rest
Sat	Cycle 20–30mins on flat terrain (or indoors). Make any position changes afterwards to improve comfort.	Cycle 20–35mins on flat terrain. Aim to ride relaxed and learn how the bike works and feels.	Cycle 30–40mins on flat terrain. Make any position changes afterwards to improve comfort.	Cycle 20–30mins on flat terrain. Add a 10-minute run after the bike.
Sun	Rest	Rest	Rest	Rest

	Week 5	Week 6	Week 7	Week 8
Mon	Swim 25 mins. Alternate 1, 2, then 3 lengths. Keep count of total.	Swim 25–35 mins. Alternate 1, 2, 3, then 4 lengths at a time. Keep count of total.	Swim 25–35 mins. Alternate 1, 2, 3, then 4 lengths at a time. Keep count of total.	Swim 20 mins. Single lengths only. Count your strokes per length and stay smooth. Keep count of total.
Tues	Rest	Rest	Rest	Rest
Wed	Run 20–25 mins Alternate walk 1-min, run 1-min.	Run 25–30 mins. Alternate walk 1-min, run 1-min.	Run 25–30 mins. Alternate walk 1-min, run 2-mins.	Run 15 mins. Alternate walk 1-min, run 1-min.
Thurs	Rest	Rest	Rest	Rest
Fri	Rest	Rest	Rest	Rest
Sat	Cycle 20–30mins on flat terrain (or indoors). Make any position changes afterwards to improve comfort.	Cycle 20–35mins on flat terrain. Aim to ride relaxed and learn how the bike works and feels.	Cycle 30–45mins on flat terrain. Make any position changes afterwards to improve comfort.	Cycle 20–30mins on flat terrain. Feel the pressure on the pedals and relax the upper body. Add a 10-minute run after the bike.
Sun	Extra session in your weakest sport	Extra session in your weakest sport	Extra session in your weakest sport	Extra session in your weakest sport

Note: After 8 weeks you can revert to week one, adding 5 or 10 minutes on to sessions. It is enough to swim for 40-60 mins, cycle 60-90 mins and run 30-60 mins at the very most in your first winter. You can also add another session on Tuesday or Thursday.

Build up slowly

This plan can seem very easy and can be completed without breaking sweat. However, deep inside your muscles, joints and blood, there are many changes afoot, so you must proceed slowly. Get too much done too soon and you will end up injured or suffer burn out very quickly. Enjoy a slow build up of the quantity and frequency of training; much in your life is about to change for the better.

Getting base started

If you have a background in endurance sports and a good fitness level, you can build slightly faster. Ex-runners can reduce their normal mileage whilst cyclists can reduce cycle frequency. Ex-swimmers need to learn biking while running slowly.

	Week 1	Week 2	Week 3	Week 4
Mon	Swim 15–30 mins. Single lengths with rest between. Keep count of total.	Swim 30–35 mins. Single lengths with rest between. Keep count of total.	Swim 40–45 mins. Single lengths with occasional double-lengths. Keep count of total.	Swim 20–25 mins. Single lengths with rest between. Keep count of total.
Tues	Your choice day: do a favourite session or route that makes you feel good and love training.	Your choice day: do a favourite session or route that makes you feel good and love training.	Your choice day: do a favourite session or route that makes you feel good and love training.	Your choice day: do a favourite session or route that makes you feel good and love training.
Wed	Run 20–25 mins. Start easy with walk, jog, then run. Stay relaxed and loose in the upper body.	Run 25–35 mins. Start easy with walk, jog, then run. Do this as your warm up in all future sessions and races.	Run 40–45 mins, relaxed and feeling good at the end, not exhausted.	Run 20–25 mins. It may be shorter but keep your form relaxed and your breathing steady.
Thurs	Extra session in your weakest sport. Concentrate on good technique and work on something you have a lot to gain from.	Extra session in your least favoured sport. Whilst training think why you do not like it and how to make things more fun in the future.	Extra session in your weakest sport. Concentrate on good technique and work on something you have a lot to gain from.	Extra session in your least favoured sport. Whilst training think why you do not like it and how to make things more fun in the future.
Fri	Rest	Rest	Rest	Rest
Sat	Cycle 40–60 mins on flat terrain (or indoors). Make any position changes afterwards to improve comfort.	Cycle 60–75 mins on flat terrain. Aim to ride relaxed and learn how the bike works and feels.	Cycle 80–90 mins on flat terrain. Make position changes afterwards to improve comfort.	Cycle 50 mins on flat terrain. Add a 10-minute run after the bike.
Sun	Rest	Rest	Another session in your weakest sport.	Rest

	Week 5	Week 6	Week 7	Week 8
Mon	Swim 25–35 mins. Alternate 1, 2, then 3 lengths. Focus on drills that make you smooth.	Swim 35–45 mins. Alternate 1, 2, 3, then 4 lengths. Keep count of total.	Swim 45 mins. Alternate 1, 2, 3, then 4 lengths. Keep count of total.	Swim 25–30 mins. Alternate 1, 2, then 3 lengths. Focus on drills that make you smooth.
Tues	Your choice day: do a favourite session or route that makes you feel good and love training.	Rest	Your choice day: do an endurance day in your strongest sport.	Rest
Wed	Run 25 mins. Start easy with walk, jog, then run. Stay relaxed and loose in the upper body. Run 35–45 mins	Start easy with walk, jog, then run. Do this as your warm up in all future sessions and races.	Run your longest run yet by at least 10 mins. Stay relaxed and feeling good at the end, not exhausted.	Run 20–30 mins. It may be shorter but keep your form relaxed and your breathing steady.
Thurs	Extra session in your weakest sport. Concentrate on good technique and work on something you have a lot to gain from.	Extra session in your least favoured sport. Try a new route or session to make it fun.	Extra session in your weakest sport. Concentrate on good technique.	Extra session in the sport done least in the past 3 weeks.
Fri	Rest	Rest	Rest	Rest
Sat	Cycle 60 mins on flat terrain (or indoors). Make note of elements you need to work on (e.g. out of the saddle riding).	Cycle 75 mins on flat terrain. Aim to ride relaxed and vary the gearing to see what works best for you.	Cycle 90 mins on rolling terrain. Make any position changes afterwards to improve comfort or handling.	Cycle 50 mins on flat terrain, spinning an easy gear to make the legs feel light, not heavy, afterwards. Add a 10-minute run after the bike.
Sun	Rest	Rest	Another session in your weakest sport. Keep thinking about good technique and being relaxed.	Rest

Note: After 8 weeks, revert to week one, adding 10–30 per cent on sessions to increase the endurance training effect. More frequent training can be done but do not train too often: the third week should always be the hardest with the fourth week the easiest. Ex-swimmers and cyclists can swim two to three times what is shown. Runners can do up to twice the run duration shown.

Springtime

After the steady base building of winter, spring marks a change in the length of the days and your fitness. By March or April, winter is long gone and you can train faster with no extra effort.

Bridging the gap

To bridge the gap between the emergence of spring and your first races, your training starts to have harder efforts and more event-specific sessions. This is an ideal time to plan to do some events in the single sports and set your own training time trial efforts.

Spring is the ideal time to start incorporating more moderate to high intensity work in order to prepare for the first events of the season.

	Week 1	Week 2	Week 3	Week 4
Mon	Swim 25–35 mins. Faster work over 4–8 lengths. Focus on faster swimming but staying smooth.	Swim 35–45 mins. Alternate fast efforts over 1, 2, 3, then 4 lengths with easy 2-length drill recoveries between.	Swim 45 mins. After a warm up of 10–15 mins of 1, 2, 3, lengths, swim a time trial over 400m. Finish off with 500m of drill work. Keep a note of your TT time.	Swim 25–30 mins. Alternate 1, 2, then 3 lengths. Focus on drills that make you smooth.
Tues	Rest	Rest	Your choice day: do an endurance day in your strongest sport.	Rest
Wed	Run 25–30 mins. Start easy with walk, jog, then run. Include 200m of faster running every 2–3 minutes but keep relaxed. Cool down with 3 mins walking.	Run 35–45 mins. Start easy with walk, jog, then run for 10–15 mins. Do this as your warm up in all future sessions and races.	Run your longest run yet by at least 10 mins. Be relaxed and feeling good at the end, not exhausted.	Run 20–30 mins. It may be shorter but keep your form relaxed and your breathing steady.
Thurs	Extra session in your weakest sport. Concentrate on technique.	Extra session in your least favoured sport. Whilst training think why you do not like it and how to make things more fun in the future.	Extra session in your weakest sport. Concentrate on good technique and work on something you have a lot to gain from.	Extra session in your least favoured sport. Whilst training think why you do not like it and how to make things more fun in the future.
Fri	Rest	Rest	Rest	Rest
Sat	Cycle 60 mins. After a 10–15 minute warm up use bigger than normal gears on inclines to build strength. Make a note of gears used and where.	Cycle 75 mins on flat terrain. Aim to ride relaxed but with a high cadence (>95rpm).	Cycle 90 mins on rolling terrain. Try riding the uphills relaxed, the flat sections as fast as possible and the downhills smooth and confident.	Cycle 50 mins on flat terrain spinning an easy gear to make legs feel light, not heavy afterwards. Change and run for 10–20 mins very easy.
Sun	Your choice endurance day: use a favourite route or pool. Keep the effort relaxed.	Cycle + run 'bricks' 50–60mins. Spin an easy gear 10 mins, then run for 10 mins very easy. Back to the bike and repeat.	Another session in your weakest sport. Keep thinking about good technique and being relaxed.	Rest

Note: After 4 weeks you can add extra time, effort or even two sessions in a day to ensure the second 4-week period gives further improvements in fitness.

Summer: the race season

From May or June, the racing season is underway and you have maximum daylight. Don't eliminate all longer sessions; ensure you get race-specific training that works towards your goals.

Getting race ready

Here are some useful training sessions to help you get race ready. You can also use the spring and winter sessions listed earlier for endurance or variety. If you are not going fast, you need to be going easy and thinking about developing good technique.

	Swim	**Bike**	**Run**	**Extras**
Speed	**Swim 45 mins** Warm up: 15 mins technique drills. Main session: 200m efforts at race pace with 30 secs recovery between. Aim to start with 5 and add 1 or 2 each time you do this session. Cool down: relaxed 400m.	**Cycle 50-60 mins** on rolling terrain. Warm up: 15 mins easy riding Main session: 3 min efforts at race pace with 30 secs spin recovery between. Aim to start with 4 and add 1 or 2 each time you do this session. Cool down: relaxed flat section spinning.	**Run 35 mins** Warm up: easy jog Run at normal pace for 3 mins and then accelerate for 2 mins. Aim to keep it smooth but moving with a fast leg cadence Repeat until form goes or you've done 25 mins. Cool down: 5-8 min jog.	**Cycle 50-60 mins** on hilly terrain. Warm up: 15 mins easy riding on flat. Main session: practise hill descents to see how your braking and cornering can make you faster. Aim to find the hilliest, most twisty route you can. Cool down: relaxed flat section spinning.
Speed	**Swim 45 mins** Warm up: 15 mins technique drills. Main session: 100, 200, 50, 300m race pace with 30 secs recovery between. Aim to start with 1 or 2; eventually do 3 sets. Cool down: relaxed 400m.	**Cycle 50-60 mins** on hilly terrain. Warm up: 15 mins easy riding on flat. Main session: hill efforts at faster than race pace with spin recovery on flats or downhills. Aim to find hilliest route you can. Cool down: relaxed flat section spinning.	**Run 35 mins** Warm up: easy jog 10 mins. Main session: 2-3 mins hill efforts at faster than race pace with jog down recovery. Find a 400m hill or a rolling route. Cool down: easy relaxed 5-8 mins jog.	**Swim 45 mins** (use as an easy day). Warm up: 10 mins technique drills. Main session: practise push off's, turns and getting out of the pool fast. Find the smoothest and fastest ways that work for you. Cool down: relaxed 300m.

	Swim	Bike	Run	Extras
Race specific	**Swim 30 mins** Warm up: 20 mins technique drills and smooth swimming. Main session: 50m fast then 20 secs recovery followed by 300m time trial. Easy swim 5 mins, then repeat. Cool down: relaxed 400m.	**Cycle 60 mins** Warm up: 10–15 mins. Main session: move to bigger normally used gears. Aim to ride at race speed for 15–20 mins. Cool down: relaxed flat section spinning, then run for 10–20 mins relaxed.	**Run 35 mins** Warm up: easy running but include 200m of faster running every 3 mins. Main session: run for 21 mins, progressively faster every 7 mins. Cool down: 5–8 mins jog.	**Cycle + run 'bricks' 50–60 mins** Warm up: spin an easy gear 10 mins. Main session: ride fast for approx. 20 mins. Transition and run 10 mins very fast. Cool down: 10 mins jog.
Variety	**Swim 35–45 mins** Warm up: 400m smooth continuous. Main session: alternate fast front crawl 100's with 50m easy breaststroke. Feel the water; don't watch the clock. Cool down: relaxed 300m.	**Cycle 45 mins** on flat terrain. Aim to ride relaxed but with a high cadence (>95rpm). Look to find at what rpm you can no longer pedal smooth. Try to raise this with regular spinning sessions.	**Run 30 mins** Warm up: easy running. Main session: throughout the run include 200m fast efforts whenever you feel ready and able to do so: keep smooth. Cool down: 5–8 mins running relaxed and breathing deeply.	**Multiple bricks** Warm up: 15 mins on bike, then jog easy for 5 mins. Main session: 4 x (4 mins Cycle + 3 mins Run). See how you go in trying some fast transitions. Cool down: 10 mins easy gear spinning.

Using your race equipment in training ensures that you know everything works correctly and how it feels to go fast.

Tapering

Reducing your training volume and getting focused on races are the keys to tapering for a peak performance. If you are still doing everything the same as normal, then you are not tapering and you cannot expect to achieve extraordinary results.

Why taper?

In some instances, you may want to enjoy good weather, use a race for training or just get fitness while you have the time. This means you won't taper but will train more, and that's fine. If you reduce training for every event, you can soon lose fitness because you are always resting or recovering. Only taper if you have been doing a consistent volume of training and the race means something to you.

How to taper

It's a personal choice how much to taper, but the concept relies on your backing off on total training time but going faster in some sessions leading up to the event. For many triathletes, this may mean a fast swim, bike and run spread over the last seven to ten days. Other sessions are a bit shorter and you feel more energetic as the event looms.

Bad tapering

Doing too little can make you feel uncoordinated, lethargic and unable to compete. Resting the day before is often a mistake as it's a great time to do a short swim or bike session and practise technical skills. You don't forget how to run, so this is less important but it may be the easiest discipline to

integrate into a hectic schedule. The mental side of tapering is to stay focused, relaxed and not doubt yourself. Negative feelings often emerge as race week starts, so be positive, let your training prove you can do the event and keep away from people with a negative mindset.

Some short but moderate to fast sessions will give you that edge in the last days before a race.

The perfect taper

Your life is ever changing and no week is exactly the same as another. However, in order to control how you feel for future races, learn from each taper what sessions work best, what is too hard (or too easy) and how you can stay positive. You may change distances but you can always use your taper experience in the future. Again, it has been proven that writing things down and reviewing them later pays big dividends.

Recovery from racing

If you have given your all in a race, you can expect to feel sore, tired and a bit down afterwards. The effects will usually peak after 48 hours but you need to know what to do and how to get back into training before too much time elapses.

must know

Your strength is already helping you to become a triathlete, but only if you focus your time and effort into the new or weak sports. You are attempting to become a jack of all trades, master of none.

Racing causes damage

Racing pushes your muscles hard, especially on the run section, so you will probably experience some soreness and possibly tight muscles for several days afterwards. You can help to reduce this by getting

From the moment you cross the finishing line, you need to start thinking about recovery, but let your body tell you when it's ready to resume full training. Swimming is easy on the muscles and is ideal soon after an event and for the next 24 to 48 hours.

in cold water immediately after racing and then once a day for the next two or three days. You are also likely to feel tired but it was good to race and now you need to recover and build back slowly.

Have a plan

If you do the complete race, no matter what your time, you must have a plan of what you will do for the first three to five days afterwards. If not, after a bad race you can be tempted to go into immediate training to punish yourself for not competing well. If you only complete part of it, say, you puncture, then there will be less run damage and you can get back into training sooner.

The golden rule

The golden rule is: the longer the race the longer the recovery. It would be wise to take it easy for one day for each mile of the run, so, on this basis, a four-mile run means four days very easy. In the table below, you can get a good idea of how an effective post-race plan would work.

must know

Missed sessions and races cannot be got back. You must plan your gradual progress and embrace the fact that you are now back to being able to train. This can be overlooked, but during your comeback thank your maker that you are well enough and have the time to do this wonderful sport.

Sun	Mon	Tues	Wed	Thurs	Fri
RACE	**Swim 25-35 mins** Relaxed with no concern about pace. Think positive thoughts and about the good parts of the race.	**Cycle 60 mins** on flat terrain (or indoors) Make a mental note of the elements you need to work on from the race, such as fast riding downhill. Note them down afterwards.	**Run 25 mins** Start easy with walk, jog, then running. Stay relaxed and loose in the upper body. Do a head to toe for tight muscles and massage them afterwards.	**Swim 25-40 mins** Alternate 1, 2, then 3 lengths. Focus on drills that make you smooth. Practise any elements you feel you got wrong in the race.	**Choice day** If fatigued, then have a rest day. The weekend can be back to normal, so use this day to recharge and maybe get your race day equipment sorted and ready.

Coming back from lay off

We may think that we'll be consistent for ever but life gets in the way. Illness, a freak injury, a heavy workload or a major life event can disrupt a training routine and interfere with the best-made plans. At some time you will have to come back from lay off.

must know

Studies suggest that total bed rest has effects after two to four weeks. Other data shows that dramatically reducing training starts to reduce fitness after four to six weeks. So do what little you can and you will cling onto most of the fitness you've built up.

All (fitness) is not lost

More often than not, except in very long lay offs, less fitness is lost than you might think. You feel fat, out of shape and very uncoordinated, but fear not that all is by any means lost. Most importantly, you must remember where you are when you start the comeback trail. Try to forget the sessions you peformed during the good times; they will come back, but leave such distances and efforts for a few weeks yet. Start small and you will build back in the time that your body allows you – too much too soon and you'll only go backwards.

Start small

There is no absolute, but start small, possibly along the lines of the beginners' programme (see page 110). When all goes well for a week, move a step up the progression ladder. If this means that it takes two to four weeks to be back on schedule, so be it. You cannot make up for lost time or beat the system.

If you have been stopped by lack of time, work or a family situation, it is less likely that you need to worry about your health compared to those people recovering from illness or an injury. In all instances, listen to your body, be patient and try not to make up for lost time or catch up with lost sessions.

Opposite: after a lay off, start back slowly, concentrating on your technique and enjoyment.

On the road

For many triathletes, being on the road means training in gyms, unfamiliar surroundings or hooking up with groups they bump into. If you do travel a lot, you can still have effective training and stick close to a plan but you have to be hyper-flexible.

What's on offer?

There is usually a fitness suite within most hotels or a fitness facility nearby. With a treadmill, a pool and cycle machines you have all you need. Running outdoors is an easy option, but you will have to ensure that the area is safe. You only need your run shoes, shorts and a top. The pool may be short but you can still get a feel for the water. The bike may not be like your road bike but get the seat height right and your legs won't know the difference. Just do what you can with the facilities on offer.

What to do

Moving from treadmill to gym bike and back again is a great 'brick' session. Just add some background music or your iPod and you can stay entertained for an hour or more. Spending 20 or 40 minutes in a short pool working on your stroke still counts even if you have no more than a dozen strokes before you reach the end. Don't do anything that imposes a sudden and high intensity effort – you could end up injured. Highly competitive spin sessions, using totally new weights machines or throwing yourself into a circuits class may be excessive. Keep to controlled sessions that come close to the equipment and workouts you normally do.

Duathlon and aquathlon

These may be two-sport rather than three-sport events but you can still use them to get a competitive fix and work on your weaknesses. One lacks a swim while the other lacks a bike, but they both contain valuable transitions and competition.

Duathlon

Often wrongly seen as a winter sport for triathletes, duathlon (run-bike-run) may be seen as harder due to two runs taking their toll. It can be used in early and late season to get race experience or for some final events before the winter base building begins again. Many events occur in the summer months, ranging from 40-minute to three-hour events. You may find running onto the bike strange, but the second run is always hard, helping you to get better at triathlon run sections. If there's one tactic you must ensure you get right, it's this: cruise the first run and be prepared to hammer the second.

Aquathlon

Swim-run events, with no permissions needed to use the roads and many venues, are becoming more popular. Many feature wetsuit open-water swims, though the opportunity to run fast after a hard swim makes many triathletes realize that this is a hard sport. Some triathlon clubs run swim-run events in the mid summer at the end of their swim sessions. This gives everyone the chance to do a time trial in the pool (200–500m usually) and then a 3–5k run effort. Suggest this as a way to make some summer sessions very race specific and fun.

want to know more?

• **For advice on racing and training for related events, look at:**
Training and Racing Biathlons, Mark Sisson (Primal Urge Press)
The Complete Guide to Duathlon Training, Hottenrott (Meyer & Meyer Sports Books)
Biathlon: Training and Racing Techniques, Souza & Babbitt (McGraw-Hill/Contemporary)
Consistent Winning, Sandler & Lobstein (Rodale Fitness)
• **Search for duathlon and aquathlon events at britistriathlon.org**

8 Completing and competing

Many people train in all three sports but rarely, sometimes never, actually get to complete a triathlon. The name seems daunting, almost super-human, but it is actually only a swim, then a bike, then a run. If you sign up for an event, train right and you too can finish a triathlon. With more races, experience and some extra effort, you could even find yourself competing, not just completing.

Choosing an event

Although some people start with long-distance races to prove that they can do the big stuff first time out, for most budding triathletes, starting with sprint triathlons is a better first footing. Smaller events are more numerous, often closer to hand and they need not take up all weekend or your life.

Choose your distance

Initially, sprint or super-sprint events in pools are the best distances to enter (sprint is 0.75, 20, 5k, whereas supersprint can be as short as 0.2, 10, 2k). You get to try the sport, without the need for an expensive wetsuit, open water practice or lots of endurance. Most beginners finish sprint events in 60–100 minutes, no longer than a half marathon takes for many, and a lot less leg soreness afterwards. Look out for events nearby and check out their details online or with local athletes/sports shops. When you are happy that an event is right for you, it's time to sign the dotted line.

Get entries in the post

I have never found a more motivating action for athletes than when they put an entry form in the post, or enter online. The reality that they are going to do a triathlon now has an exact date, a time and a distance to aim for. With no goal in mind, many people can go for months or even years without competing. They are theoretical triathletes, scaring themselves from competing, whilst others enjoy both training and racing.

Perhaps you only want to do three events a year

and spread them out, but you do need something tangible to work toards and complete. An actual finishing time, position, finisher's T-shirt and race photo make your being a triathlete a reality. This motivates even the most self-critical of athletes.

Think about logistics

As many sprint races can be over-subscribed and full in a matter of days, you have to think ahead. The event may be months away but when you enter you have to think about travelling arrangements, whether you need accommodation and whether you need to take the family along for the day. If you keep local and small scale at first, many of the hassles of travelling and, as some large races require, putting your bike in the day before the race, don't materialize.

Do your paper work early and pop it in the postbox, so that you can focus on training and building up to your events.

Race week

As Monday looms, the realization that the race is just a few days away often scares athletes into making rash decisions about training and equipment. At this point, you need a solid plan and to stay cool. There's little extra conditioning or coordination that you can gain now – you just have to stay calm and keep relaxed.

Keep the training fun and relaxed in the build up to a race. There is no need for you to feel stressed or apprehensive. You are ready!

Have a plan

You need to have some training sessions that keep your hand in each sport and allow a strong and energetic feeling by the time that race day dawns. No heroics, just modest sessions that keep you in touch with the water, your bike and the feeling of running relaxed. The logistics of equipment is central to the week. It's not about training so much as getting yourself prepared. On the opposite page, you can view a plan of what to do.

The fourth discipline

Races may theoretically be in good weather, and promotional shots often include the sun, but in many events you will have to battle against the elements. The weather could be hot, windy, cool, raining or even all of the above. Be prepared and check the expected weather in advance on a range of websites, such as www.metcheck.com, or on your local TV channel or radio station. This may affect what you pull on after the swim, how long the event will take or even how mentally harder it could be. Like a good boyscout, be prepared.

Mon	Tues	Wed	Thurs	Fri	Sat	Sun
A session in your weakest sport Work on good technique that can help you on race day. ——— Keep it relaxed and do not think about speed or trying too hard. ——— Self massage your legs, arms and shoulders for 15 mins.	**Swim 45 mins** ——— Warm up: 15 mins technique drills. ——— Main session: 100, 200, 50, 300 m race pace with 30 secs recovery in between. Aim to start with 1 or 2, eventually do 3 sets. ——— Cool down: relaxed 400m.	**Cycle 60 mins** on flat terrain (or indoors). ——— Keep it smooth but do try to include some efforts for approx. 2–3 mins with at least 1-minute recovery spinning between. ——— If any problems with the bike, get them sorted yourself or get it to a bike shop in the next 48 hours.	**Run 25 mins** Start easy with 10 mins of walk, jog, then run. ——— Run at fast but relaxed effort for approx. 2–3 mins, jog easy for 30 secs, then repeat 2–4 times. ——— Warm down: jog easy for 5 mins. ——— Nutrition: for the next three days eat regular, high-carb meals and drink at least 2 litres of water.	**Rest** Get logistics finalized, pack your kit bag and ensure everything is ready for the big day. ——— Eat well today, more than you would on a normal rest day with plenty of fluids, and relax. ——— Do not over-think about the race; just enjoy your day but do not be overly ambitious with the extra time you may have. ——— Self massage your legs for 15 mins.	**Swim 30 mins am.** ——— Warm up: 15 mins technique drills. ——— Main session: 4–6 100m race pace efforts with 15–30 secs recovery. Aim to swim them strong but not go overboard. ——— **Cycle 20–30 mins** checking out the gears, tyres and brakes. ——— **Run 10–15 mins steady** after the bike or later in the day. Add some 100m race pace efforts but keep relaxed.	Race

Which taper is best?

As you do more events you will know exactly what taper works best for you. If spare time is limited, stay positive and do short sessions. At this point it's more about getting to the event relaxed than doing any last-minute beasting sessions. The priority is swim, bike, then run. The more technical sports need practice whereas running is natural.

Race build up

When the alarm goes off on race morning, don't be scared – be excited. You have an event to do, you are all prepared and you can't wait to swim, bike and run. Well, that's the theory, but what happens in practice may differ slightly. Think ahead and you will be in a position to enjoy every event you do.

must know

Warming up increases the ability to use your muscles efficiently and makes it mentally easier to lock into race pace. The more specific the action, the easier the swim, bike and run will feel. Whatever your least coordinated sport is, do ensure that it is part of your warm up.

The night before the morning

It is easy to overeat at what feels like your 'last supper'. You have tapered your training and been eating regularly, so eat a normal-sized meal, not a carbo-loading pig-out. Have your alarm set early and know where you're going – do this the night before. Even if you do not sleep well, losing a few hours' sleep won't have much impact on your race performance. Go to bed when you feel tired and just try to relax, not worry about tomorrow.

Travelling

Allow plenty of time to drive to the location and an hour to get set up, warmed up and up to speed with any last-minute route changes. Eat before you leave or snack as someone else drives, but leave at least two hours between taking solid foods and the race. This may take some testing in training, but once you find your perfect pre-race nutrition, stick to it.

Race warm up

At the very least, you need to have warmed muscles and a brain that's ready to work on demand. Some people prefer to do an easy jog around the race location, whereas others go for a short bike ride or even a light spin on their indoor trainer by the car. Around 10–20 minutes should be enough, but do not ignore your upper body, which will be used in the swim when the gun goes off. Upper body warm ups can be achieved using resistance bands looped around a tree, fence or car towing hook – light exercise to get the blood circulating is enough. If you are very lucky, a lane or second pool will be available for warming up. If it's an open water event, you will have a set time to warm up in the water.

Transition areas are often busy and full of expensive equipment. Set out your equipment at the correct place, walk through the 'swim-in' and 'run-out' routes and then warm up.

Final preparation

A lot of time and effort goes into being competent and ready for the event in which you are about to participate. You may be at the event and warmed up but you also need to take time to prepare your transitions and know the tricky parts of the course.

Know the route you will take from the swim to your bike. It may be different from how you got to the pool in the first place.

Registration

Some triathletes prefer to register and then warm up; for others, it is the other way around. You may receive your race numbers by post or may have to pick them up on the day. If so, this is your chance to ask any questions and ensure you are happy with any rules or areas of concern about the race details.

Knowing the race route

You can never know too much about the race route. Small changes to turnaround points, in/out funnels and a lapped course mean you must be a cerebral athlete. Far too many people have missed laps or gone off course through not paying attention to the race details or maps at race registration. Don't let this happen to you.

Thinking through T1 and T2

Walk your bike to transition and take note of the swim to bike route, bike out, bike in and run out direction. With a few hundred people all trying to get through transition and the red mist of racing in your eyes, you need to be clear about what you are doing. Transition time is never an excuse to explain why you did not go faster; it's part of knowing your event. So set up your transition area, ensuring you have a helmet, run shoes, bike shoes (if applicable) and any nutrition in place. Walk through the ins and outs and ask any questions of nearby marshals.

Last-minute nerves

Once you have set up your transition and warmed up, you need to get to the swim start area. You may be all nerves but just try to stay calm, think yourself through the event and be happy that you have got this far. Most people never enter a triathlon though some do and fail to turn up due to nerves. You're on the start line, ready to go, so be positive and enjoy it. Think smooth effort and, if you have time, visualize yourself going through each part of the course.

Rack your bike with your helmet, bike shoes and other equipment in the positions that you have practised changing.

Pace your race

With little or no experience of what a triathlon feels like, it's easy to get scared by unnecessary details and ignore the things that matter. If you know what is likely to happen, you can prepare yourself mentally and get your race effort close to optimal.

must know

As the finishing line finally looms into view, the pain will disappear and jubilation appears. Savour this moment and remember all the hard work and sacrifices you and others gave to get here. You have just completed a triathlon!

Swim

With anything from 200 to 750m, but most likely 400m, to swim, it's the shortest element in the triathlon but the one where over-exertion can spoil the rest of your race. Start conservatively, ensuring you hit the 200m mark still in control, smooth and breathing controlled. Be prepared to swim your race, but draft (swim close behind another athlete to save energy) if someone is in front doing just the right speed. Overtaking can be more effort for little gain, so hold back unless the swimmer in front really is going too slow. With two laps to go, you'll be shown a 2-TO-GO board; there's no need to sprint from here – just get ready for the very hard haul out.

T1

As you tear your goggles off, start thinking about where your bike is. Run fast but stay relaxed and keep your breathing under control. Helmet and shoes on, un-rack the bike and off you go, only mounting once you pass the mount line.

Bike

As the human traffic gets busy both in transition and as you head onto the road, it's vital to stay alert, wary of other road traffic and mindful of the route.

Start off in comfortable gears, keeping the cadence smooth and applying pressure in a smooth but powerful fashion. It often takes five to ten minutes to get into a rhythm, so just stay smooth and use the gears to keep your legs spinning. Expect some fatigue in your legs by the end of the ride, but spin if they are getting tired – do not push a big gear.

T2

As you dismount and run/walk to your racking position, your legs may feel stiff and slightly wobbly. Rack the bike, helmet off, run shoes on and get out of transition smoothly with some short, fast strides.

Run

Expect the shock of triathlon to hit you as you exit transition. Tired, dead-legs and a sudden increase of breathing rate indicate you're on the run. Keep your head still, your arms setting a good rhythm.

Be sure to pace the first part of your swim to ensure you do not fatigue and lose form suddenly.

As you start the run, take some fluid to wet your throat or douse over your head to cool you down.

Swim tips

Everyone is nervous, raring to race and keen not to waste time. Although it is actually such a small part of the race, the swim section needs to be thought out and executed precisely. You will have to get to *terra firma* quickly but without wasting energy.

must know

Each discipline has its own time or 'split' that the race organizers time. This may include transition times, or the swim, bike and run may be separate to your T1 and T2 times. Making comparisons between races may be hard when there is no set place to time you at and the distances and courses differ so much.

Pacing

Your efforts in the final days before a race give you an idea of how fast you can swim. Keep yourself on the right pace and do not over-exert because of nerves. If the first 100m does not feel relaxed and easy, you've gone off too fast.

Overtaking

In pools, you overtake down the middle or tap the person in front on the foot and they (should) move over at the next turn. Don't waste energy fighting in the water – stay smooth and keep your race in mind.

Counting

To get the pacing right, count your lengths. It's your responsibility to know how far you have gone, even though lap counters will tell you when to get out. When they indicate two laps to go, think about where your bike is and the route you'll take to get to it.

Out of the pool

You will experience some dizziness as you go from horizontal to vertical. You may have to drop your swimming hat by the lap counter, but, whatever the format, falling over by running too fast at this point can cause injury and a DNF (Did Not Finish).

Opposite: Take time to practise heaving yourself out of the pool – it's a very visible part of your race prowess and you can waste valuable time if you flounder.

Bike tips

The bike is the longest distance and time of all the disciplines in a triathlon. You will be warmed up already from the swim but you need to transfer your body from a swimmer into a biker with the least effort and as quickly as possible.

must know

Riding a bike as fast as the best age groupers takes training, practice and some expensive equipment. It's the most technological part of the race and you will need many races to feel like you have mastered it.

To and fro

As abilities across the sports vary, you may catch up with fast swimmers who are slow in transition. Conversely, a poor swimmer but experienced transitioner may fly by you. You may overtake people or be overtaken yourself at any point from the edge of the pool to the bike dismount line.

Personal rhythm

Once out of transition, focus on your pedalling rhythm. You cannot draft behind other riders but you can pass them or try to keep them in sight if they pass you. As rules change over time, be sure you know how close is too close. It's your race and cheating is not the way to achieve anything worthwhile.

Traffic

You and other traffic around you will be moving at great speed. It may be a race but you need to stay within your safety zone of speed and bike handling. This may be the first time you've ridden these roads, so be aware of your fellow cyclists and stay safe.

Overtaking

If you do catch the slower riders, always give them plenty of space. If they move out suddenly to miss a

hole or drain, you could easily hit them. Ensure that it's safe to go round them by checking behind you first and then get by as quickly as you can.

This biker is in full flow on her aerobars. Prepare in training for other athletes and road traffic which will be around you as you race. Always go fast but be safe.

Gearing-down

When you are within a mile of the end of the bike course, go into a slightly easier gear and just spin. Think ahead if you are going to dismount shoeless and know where your run shoes will be waiting.

Run tips

It's the last, the hardest and most feared element of a triathlon. However, the run section means you are two-thirds of the way home and in the simplest mode of movement. You can do it – just keep moving forwards and remember the following tips.

must know

Triathlon running is just running after a bike ride. The more you do these bike-run 'brick' sessions, and run after your longer bike rides and races, the easier it will become. You may even end up liking it.

Watch the cramps

Moving from bike to run, bending down to take shoes off and putting on another pair on, can cause cramps. Make your movements carefully and don't expect too much too soon from legs that are tiring and changing disciplines.

Shorten the stride

A useful trick – and one that many competitors do the complete opposite of – is to shorten your stride early on in the run. Your hamstrings will be tight after the limited movement on the bike, so think fast feet rather than long strides.

The more times that you practise climbing off the bike and then running, the easier it will get.

It will hurt and confuse

The run hurts everyone, but some people go faster and get it over quicker. Stay positive, and walk if you need to. You don't have to run all the way, especially if there are steep hills or you get muscle cramps.

Arm rhythm counts

The key to keeping going is using your arms to dictate to your legs. Focus on keeping your arms moving in a rhythm and breathing deeply. Your legs will follow and you'll focus on what you can control. Try and keep your arms and shoulders relaxed.

As you exit T2 it is best to be relaxed. Your legs may feel strange but this sensation will disappear in a matter of minutes. Smile and it feels easier instantly.

Recovering from racing

Racing takes its toll, due to extra effort on the day and because of the stress of moving between sports at speed. You've done a tri, and it's time to give your body some R & R, so it may repair and grow stronger from the event – treat yourself.

must know

Research on massage may not show that processes like blood flow or toxin removal are greatly enhanced, but the personal experience of many athletes is that it works to keep them healthy and less injury prone.

Immediate damage limitation

Muscles will most likely be sore, but if a post-race massage is on offer, get one – you'll recover faster and treat yourself. Eating and rehydration are your first priority after packing everything away – some people experience headaches after racing due to dehydration and poor nutrition. Don't let this happen to you. Go with what your body tells you it wants.

Highs and lows

After the high of finishing a race, many triathletes can feel a bit low or even deflated for a few days afterwards. This may be due to the effort of racing. Always have another event planned a month or so later for you to work towards.

Start easy

The first days of training after races have to be easy, low impact and entail listening to any aches or pains that you have. Even if another event is coming up very soon, you need to give your body enough time to repair itself and not break it down further. Think about fun sessions, practising skill work with a modest amount of time rather than the maximum amount of time you can spare. Maybe use the time to train with friends keen to follow you into triathlon.

Recovery after racing can be improved by correct hydration. Make sure that you replace lost fluid even after training sessions.

Race analysis

With three sports, varying race distances and courses, triathlons offer us new opportunities to learn and improve. Whether you've just completed your first, fifth or fifty-fifth race, you can learn from the experience and grow through detailed post-race analysis.

Post mortem

After a race, look honestly at your strengths and weaknesses. Analyse the opportunities and threats to improving further. You may go up-distance, enter more races or go for PB's in events in which you have already competed. Don't stagnate or live on the successes of past races. The future holds growth and reward if you're willing to learn lessons and work hard.

Beyond the splits

As well as the times you achieved, did you enjoy the event? Did you discover something new about yourself? It's not just race times and winners that matter; it's also taking what you have learnt and applying it positively elsewhere in your life.

Cost benefit-ratio

If you've been training for 20 hours a week but seem to be going backwards in your race times, perhaps you should do less, but, ironically, end up achieving more. Conversely, if you barely scraped one session per week, don't expect to be the fastest athlete or as good as you could be. My experience tends towards a 6–10 hour ballpark for most triathletes – more if you want age group excellence but less if you just want to get round the course, not crawl round.

want to know more?

• Having a diary on your computer can make training and racing analysis must clearer than scraps of paper. A simple diary for PCs or Macs can be downloaded and tried out from www.ismarttrain.com
• A useful DVD to look at is *Triathlon Through the Eyes of the Elite* (available from Amazon)

9 Learning and growing

Triathlon is a part of your life; it is not a matter of life and death. By training for and taking part in triathlons, we can all learn more about ourselves, grow in confidence and also pass on positive benefits to the rest of our lives. If you use your training and racing positively to learn, you will end up achieving far more than just being healthy and fit.

Growing as an athlete

You have three different sports to perfect as well as many pieces of specialist equipment and sports nutrition to hone. Therefore it takes time, effort and analysis to be able to become a better triathlete and it won't happen overnight.

Small acorns

During every week, every race and almost every session, you can learn just one little thing that will make you better at the sport and improve your performance. It may be the correct hand action on entry into the water when swimming or the right way to set up your brake blocks for safe braking when cycling. There is so much to learn that you need to stop worrying about the scale of it all and relax in the knowledge that experience comes with practice and the advance of time; it must stay fun.

Confidence and competence

Each time you perfect a particular movement or understand what makes a good training session for you personally, you will grow a little more. This increase in competence also raises your confidence. You will not be a beginner forever, so enjoy the process of climbing up the learning curve.

Asking and understanding

Experienced friends, coaches or even the top triathletes you come across are all good sources for advice and won't mind answering your questions. Most people like handing on their experience, but be sure you fully comprehend what you are being

Opposite: Don't be afraid to ask any questions and discuss your problems. Experts and elite athletes are good sources of experience to tap into.

told and that it makes sense and is relevant for you at your level of fitness and expertise. Advice is only good if you understand it and it is truthful.

Write it down

It is important to learn lessons from your own experience and remember any technical advice you are given by writing it down in a special triathlon diary or journal. This can become your bible of experience which you can refer back to as and when needed. It will help to motivate you when you are feeling downhearted as well as providing useful insights into making progress. Include any helpful articles found in magazines, useful data from websites, and, of course, keep it next to this book.

The perfect week

Those perfect weeks when training and racing go well are to be cherished and capitalized upon. Although they may not happen often, sooner or later you'll have a great week of training, racing or even both, which will justify all your hard work and effort.

Life has a way

When you are training and racing as a hobby, many other priorities will come before triathlon. You have to take the rough with the smooth and keep telling yourself that you are a triathlete. There will be a good week some time in the future, and the present bad one will go easier if you think positively.

The curse of numbers

The downside of your biggest week, the longer session or the best race you have ever had is the comedown from it. Training time cannot ever expand towards a 30-hour week as you approach spending almost as much time indulging your tri-hobby as being at real-life work. Similarly, super-long sessions or peak races are followed by lesser ones. View the exceptional as just that and accept that lesser distances, speeds or totals are a reality. More is not better after a certain optimum is reached.

Planning makes perfect

Planning what you intend to do can help to increase the chances of maximizing the good weeks. Making time whilst you are on holiday to train as well as doing family stuff, DIY or sightseeing is an example of good planning. Similarly, knowing when there's

more daylight on offer, work is easing off or you have a day in lieu helps when planning a good training week. If the weather is horrendous, or you have massive family or social commitments or wall-to-wall work, it may not be the best time to plan that perfect week.

It's the total amount of training that you accrue, not any one week or any one session, that counts. Every athlete has to let life get in the way occasionally; if you don't do this, then you're taking your training too seriously. Triathlon is a lifestyle that allows you to blend your exercise and competing alongside the rest of your commitments, such as work, family and a social life – make balance your watch word.

You have to make the most of your time, so be punctual, have a plan and be flexible whenever you need to be.

Over-training

When constant over reaching leads to staleness and decreasing fitness and performance, you've become 'over-trained'. This is not only the case with people who train for 20 hours or more a week, but also with any triathlete balancing work, family and a host of other things plus trying to achieve triple-sport goals.

must know

Exercise addiction has its very own field of psychology, studying why people become fixated on training and racing. If you cannot take a day off, if everything else comes lower down your priority list than your precious sport, then you need to talk to friends and, in extreme cases, seek professional help.

Overdoing it

The downsides of exercise are rarely talked about; it's usually seen as a win, win situation. However, in the race to beat ourselves, and maybe others, too, it is easy to slide down the slippery slope of thinking that triathlon is all about who does the most. Some of you reading this may think 'I wish', but even clear-headed people can soon be doing too much in their quest to be better. Do your family, fellow athletes and friends tell you when you are doing too much? If so, heed their warning. Triathlon is play time, not a second job.

Watch for the signs

The signs that you may be doing too much training are varied but they may include such symptoms as being very irritable, lacking a sense of humour and taking yourself too seriously. Watch out also for repeated tiredness before, during and after your training sessions. You may find that you are not able to swim, bike or run anything close to your normal speed even when you are trying really hard to do so. When your effort does not pay back with a turn of speed and you are feeling very tired, it's time to back off – you are over-trained.

The cure is easy

Whilst the cause of your staleness and fatigue may be too much training on top of too many other things going on in your life, the cure is easy – just do less. Don't stop training completely as you will experience severe withdrawal symptoms, but do less sessions, for shorter periods, and keep it fun. If you have any hard group sessions or races, you may need to cancel them or just set your sights lower and see the fun-o-meter as the key to getting back to freshness.

When it gets serious

In extreme cases, people can end up with serious health complications by training themselves into extreme fatigue, especially if an underlying illness is present. You want to be healthy and enjoy life and if this happens to you, your family and training partners should already be warning you to stop or at least slow down. Again, heed their warnings.

At the end of an event or a challenging session you may be fatigued. However, if, day after day, you feel exhausted by your training, it's time to add some rest days and do light training.

Your next event

When you finish one event, it is likely that you will have another lined up to be thinking about. By using each event, you can learn and progress; it may not always be upwards – sometimes it may be sideways or even downwards – but it will be for good reasons.

must know

The British Triathlon (see page 187) lists many events to help you seek new adventures and fun things to experiment with. From Rowathlon to Quadrathlon and Aquathlon to Duathlon, there's more than just swim-bike-run to try. Some have several swim-bike-runs back to back; others are out of the usual order. Enjoy.

You never stop learning

Whether you've just completed your first triathlon or want to return to events a decade after you first did them, you should be learning a lot from every race. It may be that you are getting to grips with a new piece of equipment or finding out how you fare over a new distance. This is the fun of triathlon and the range of single sports in which you can also compete. This variety means you are never bored and you'll always be seeking knowledge.

Opportunites

A triathlon can be an event to complete, compete in or conquer. However you approach it, an event provides an opportunity to try something new, learn from the experience and become a better triathlete. It may be you are better at organizing yourself the day before, better at balancing work-life-training, or moving faster from start to finish. Even events where it all appears to go wrong still provide an opportunity to learn and put them right next time around.

Progress or enjoy?

Not every race means you will go faster or that your intention should always be to do so. Some events are there just to enjoy, perhaps as a team relay or as a good way of experiencing great scenery and an interesting course. Know what the next event is for and that you measure races for enjoyment on just that, not only the finish time or your position.

A brave new world

Many people eventually succumb to trying a longer race, e.g. moving from Sprint to Olympic distance (OD) or from OD up to Half Ironman (also known as 70.3). Alternatively, you could try your hand at other multisport events, such as Rowathlon; your next race could be a brave move into uncharted territory.

must know

At any point in your triathlon career it can help to keep your motivation and direction by listing your all-time goals list. These big plans can be an Ironman, to podium in your age group category, or another big challenge such as riding Lands End - John O'Groats. Make your goals big and they will see you through the tough times.

Multisport means that you can have fun experimenting with various sports. Look around for something new and exciting to enter, such as a Duathlon.

Getting the right balance

Learning how to balance your triathlon training, racing and aspiration can seem far away when you first enter the sport, However, it is an addictive pastime and the time has come to look at learning how to balance the sport.

must know

Most triathletes are achievers - type-A personalities who get stuff done whilst others watch. Be sure that you have goals, listed in your diary, that pertain to other things outside of triathlon. Refer to these when triathlon gets too consuming.

Prioritization

At times, you may miss training sessions, even races, due to other commitments. Learning to accept this and move on is invaluable. By taking time out from tri, you can keep things in balance and make time for the other things in life that are important to you.

End of season

This is the ideal time to recover by taking a month out. However, this doesn't mean becoming a couch potato; just back off from a regimented plan. Learn how much training you need to do to keep sane, but try to lose enough fitness to get you motivated to start your winter whilst catching up on other interests and commitments.

Find out about your reserves

Take your energy and positive outlook into other areas. Finishing and competing in triathlons is not about being fast; it can also make you a more rounded, and complete person. However, this is not the case if you take yourself too seriously, start training far too many hours and set unreasonable goals for yourself. It's good to want to excel, but it's also good to be well-rounded, not just seeing life from a tri-angle all the time.

Loves and hates

By viewing the training sessions and events in your diary, you can see what makes you tick and what makes you seethe. You may have mental blocks or hate things for good reason. Knowing this is invaluable to continued future participation in the sport.

Make it enjoyable

If you truly hate a certain session or race, don't punish yourself by making it into something you feel you must do. This is your hobby and you should what you do. At times we need to do things to take ourselves out of the comfort zone, but that's a million miles from seeing triathlon as a penance that must be made constantly hard and difficult.

Look at the sessions, people and events you love, and make these central to your future plan. The positive sense you get from these will increase the quality of your tri lifestyle. Professional athletes may be fast but they love what they do and therefore they can keep on doing it when others give up. If you love what you are doing, where's the hardship?

Challenge, not change

You can stretch your limits, achieve personal bests, maybe even finish on the podium, but you are you and will never be anyone else. Do not set too much importance on being good as an athlete – you must aim to be the best you can be. This is as worthy an achievement as those athletes who are the very best. Challenge yourself but do not believe it will make you a different person. Triathlon is your hobby, not the most important thing in your life.

want to know more?

• For futher details and information on how to grow and develop as a triathlete, see the following books: *Mental Toughness Training for Sports*, Loehr (Plume) *Serious Training for Serious Athletes*, Sleamaker (Leisure Press) *Peak Fitness for Women*, Newby (Fraser) *Smart Exercise*, Bailey (Houghton Mifflin)

10 Tips and tricks

Experienced triathletes can give you useful one-liners that often serve as mantras. These tips and tricks are ideal not only for getting things right but also as a way of remembering key concepts and things to do. You may devise your own, but in the following pages you will find some athletes' golden nuggets of advice.

Making the most of your time

Using your time both productively and efficiently is a key skill to master if you want to become a better triathlete and enjoy your training, events and the fitness they bring. Here are some expert tips that you might find useful and inspirational.

must know

You can integrate your training into weekly rhythms by thinking ahead. For example, you can find a pool site on www.swimmersguide. com so you can swim in a new location if you are travelling for work or going away on holiday. **Mark Rickinson**

Have a training plan

It makes you allocate what you need to do to the time you have available. Have a purpose for each workout – it's better to do two sessions with the right effects than three aimless ones. **Jonathan Kembery**

All in perspective

Always make the most of your time but whatever you do, don't become obsessed with triathlon, which is very easy to do. It's easy to get sucked into all the competitions and training, etc., but remember that you don't want to have a 'Triathlon Widow, Husband, Wife, Girlfriend or Boyfriend' or they may not be around for too long! **Rob Bell**

Ride to work.

It may not be scientific focused intervals sets, but you can still get a couple of hours of riding in each day to build up the miles. Try and find a safe and enjoyable route. I commute right across London through parks and along towpaths. It is a bit longer than hammering down the main roads, but it's very pleasant and still quicker than the tube! **Graham McCarthy**

Make appointments

If you are very busy, try to carefully integrate your weekly training sessions into specific calendar appointments in your diary week before the week commences (Microsoft Outlook Calendar is great for this) and try and treat these sessions like any other meeting or appointment. This way you will have a focused plan, you have carved out the time and, as a result, you are more likely to stick to it.

Lee Piercy

Training before work

This gives you more energy and takes a key thing off the 'to-do' list, especially training while commuting – run or ride to work and save time.

Jonathan Kembery

An extra inner tube

Carry one more inner tube than you would normally. It's amazing how much time this can save you, when compared to walking home.

Eamonn Sheridan

Whether you're going training or competing in a race, it's a good idea to keep some spare gear in the back of your car. You never know when you may need it.

Keep it fun and positive

Simple things sometimes make life more enjoyable for you. They can turn boredom into fun and race nerves into a smile. When there's so much focus on being good and fast as a triathlete, the best advice is to lighten up and enjoy what you are doing.

must know

When faced with an injury that prevents you from doing the training you would normally do, focus on what you can do. For example, If you can't run or bike, put some time in at the pool.

Find a training partner

Quality interval sessions are hard to do on your own, so find a training partner. For example, when we do 30-second intervals, we race against each other and adopt characters (for example, Tom Boonen versus Robbie McKewan), and we keep score as to who wins each interval. You could even wear team kit to make it more like the real thing!
Eamonn & Debbie Sheridan

Family days

Make one day at the weekend your 'family day'. Spend some quality time doing things together so that your family don't resent it when you spend the other day away from them training. Of course, the 'family day' also doubles as your rest day!
Terry Harvey

Enjoy life

It is OK to have rest days, eat junk food, binge drink every now and again even during the peak season. We are not professional athletes and I personally find it extremely therapeutic to go out drinking with my friends every couple of weeks... it makes me feel refreshed and eager to recommence my training.
Lee Piercy

The marshals

Don't forget the marshals; a wave or comment as you go past will brighten their day. My favourite is to ask poolside marshals if they are open to bribes to let me do a couple of lengths fewer – it gets a laugh if nothing else.

Chris Brown

Variety and fun

Enjoy the challenge that training programmes bring. For example, if you travel a lot for work, use this time to run and cycle and experience new places. Creating fun and variety in your programme is key.

Kate O'Neil

Get out and ride, run or swim and you will feel much better about yourself. This pastime is fun first and foremost: a chance to enjoy the outdoors and know more about yourself.

Tapering and race week

With one to two weeks to go, think about what you specifically have to do for your event in the way of training and rest. Don't do random workouts; it needs to be paced to perfection, so you hit the event confident, competent and ready to compete.

must know

It's easy to get distracted as an event draws near and you think that you have not done enough or need to buy some new equipment to help you race better. Draw up a plan of what you will do at least a week in advance, and only change equipment that needs to be changed.

Visualize future success

Winning always happens twice – once in the mind and then in the real world. Long before the race, try to clearly visualize yourself taking part in the race and transitions, winning, finishing in the top field or maybe even just completing the race. Make your dreams a reality

Dave Mather

Achieving a balance

Talk to your family about how your training sessions can best be scheduled for them in your 'big week'. And don't assume that you know when will be best without asking them first!

Mark Rickinson

Advice for vets

As a vet athlete (over 40s), you must accept that as you get older you will have to train even harder to maintain the same standard as in days gone by. You should also bear in mind that recovery will take longer. Once you have acknowledged this simple fact, you'll be better placed to set yourself realistic race targets which are based on the time you have available to train.

Terry Harvey

Getting the right mind set

I perform best when I have am relaxed and happy. Anger, confusion and discontentment are the least effective mind sets for me. Mitigate the confused mind set by good preparation and 'reccing' the course, transitions and all the race details. Forget what other people are fretting about – stay focused – but that does not mean 'being serious', which so so many athletes seem to do prior to a race. Try and feel light and relaxed; remember your pay cheque is not dependent on a good race, so there is every reason to enjoy it.

Lee Piercy

After an event, it's time to talk about what was and what could have been, and to plan the next group session or event.

At the race

When you have trained for months in preparation for this big moment, it's worth having the experience of other triathletes to help make the day go well. At the very last hurdle, you must be sure that you do the right things and not trip yourself up. Here are some useful tips from some old hands.

must know

Make transitions as simple and as routine as possible by only ever changing one thing at a time, never more, so your transition evolves. Even if you have some out and a time-saving idea, change just one thing per race. Changing too many things at once is a recipe for disaster. **Antony Birt**

Have a written time schedule

This should track back from your start time and include the times you are going to wake, eat, travel, etc. Use a non-racing partner or friend to keep an eye on the time for you.
Eammon and Debbie Sheridan

Staying warm

On early season races, try wearing a long-sleeved thermal rash vest under your tri suit. It saves time in transition trying to put on a jacket or arm warmers designed for swimming in and it also drys out quickly on the bike and keeps your core warm.
Paul Chambers

A family affair

Involve your family in the race, maybe as marshals or crew. Make the event a family day out which they all enjoy, not just something for you to do alone.
Terry Harvey

Lighten up

Try talking to your fellow competitors – they are not wild savages waiting to rip your head off. Look around at the stony faces before the start of a race

and randomly pick somebody to make a comment to. Anything will do; just try and see where it leads. I do this at every race and not once has anybody blanked me – rather, they are only too happy to lighten the atmosphere.
Chris Brown

Relaxation and focus
Know what helps you to relax/focus before a race – chatting and joking with others, warming up on your own, listening to music, checking out bits of the course, or staying with family/kids, etc.
Mark Rickinson

Be alert
Never follow the cyclist in front of you so blindly that you don't notice when they miss all the signs and go off route, causing you to do the same!
Nicky Deane-Simmons

Get to the race early to have time to set up your transition, walk through the various exit and entry points and do your warm up.

The experts

When it's been your job and you have been at the top of the pile, you know your stuff. The triathlon experts featured here cannot lend you their genes but they can give you some tried, tested and invaluable advice, so read and digest.

must know

There is a wealth of experience in books and websites. However, don't get snowed under trying to work out what people do to be great. Focused hard work reaps rewards. Choose no more than four books and websites to refer to for advice. If you prefer a new one, drop an old one from the list.

Bodywork is important

Bodywork is the triathlete's fourth discipline and just as important as the other three. To improve consistently and stay clear of injury, try to build in time each week to fit in your core work. Stretching, massage and weights and a regular periodic check up with a good chiropractor (or similar) will help ensure that all your joints and spine remain aligned.
Dr Graham Matthews, Chiropractor

Breathing

Deep breathing instantly centres you and oxygenates your body, preparing you for peak physical and mental performances. This can work for anyone during any workout. The next time you're training, or competing, breathe deeply, into your belly, and you'll feel stronger, more focused and in control.
Eric Harr, Pro Triathlete

Tapering

Of all the various aspects that go into training for an endurance event, tapering is perhaps the least understood. Despite this, the general idea is straightforward – to go into the event fresh but fit. This, of course, is the hard part.
Chuckie V, Pro Triathlete

Set goals that inspire you

Every so often, set new fresh goals that excite and inspire you. Goals that reside 'within your comfort zone' may not provide the deep-down motivation you need to lace up your running shoes and bolt outdoors for a cold winter morning run. The best way to infuse your program with passion is to vary your routine, work out with friends and strive for goals that you once thought were unattainable. Take a moment right now to write down your three triathlon-related goals – and how you plan on achieving them.

Eric Harr, Pro Triathlete

Save energy

A lot of energy is wasted by riders who are too tense on their machines. It is good practice to save energy by using only the muscles that are needed and, as such, your hands should hold the bars 'lightly'. Practise riding no-handed on your own in a traffic-free environment. Steer the bike by leaning slightly one way or the other. These sessions can be done at weekends on airfields or quiet trading estates.

Andy Cook, ex GB Cyclist

At the race

It is all too easy for the older generation to live by the old adage that stemmed from their generation 'no pain, no gain' and to keep plugging away regardless. To do this does not provide the body with adequate rest for the adaptation process to take place. Alternate hard and easy days and take an easy week comparatively every fourth week.

Andy Cook, ex GB Cyclist

Elite triathletes like Stuart Hayes look smooth because they practise being relaxed and fluid.

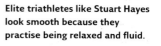

Top age groupers

To be at the front of the race, even win medals at the World Championship, you have to be dedicated and have absorbed a lot of experience. The following athletes can pass on a tip or two that may help you to achieve your own PB or beat your arch rival.

must know

Age group racing spans distances from Sprint up to Ironman and it includes triathlon, duathlon, aquathlon and quadrathlon. There are varying qualifying criteria and events that you have to know all about in order to be included and fit the selection criteria.

The three 'C's

The little mantra I use is the three 'C's:

1 Confidence: be happy you have done all the miles.

2 Control: be sure that all your equipment is in top condition, and don't blame your performance on lack of preparation.

3 Clarity: be sure you know what you want to achieve.

Sophie Whitworth

Get your priorities right

Remember who (and what) pays the bills when occasionally you are faced with the dilemma of an important planned training session and unforeseen work task or meeting. Also remember that very, very few people make any reasonable salary from being a pro (even if we were fortunate to have the genes).

Lee Piercy

Recce time is seldom wasted

Whether it is from walking through your transitions to driving the bike course or walking the run course, this time is definitely not wasted. It will ensure that you do not waste your time and energy during the race working out where you should be or how far you have to go or how steep the next hill is.

Mark Hanby

Planning your training

Think carefully about how many sessions you need to do with others, like club mates, as often training alone requires less time overall and can be done more flexibly. Don't think about going to do any training session without a clear idea of what you are going to do, for how long and why.

Mark Rickinson

Eat a varied diet

The body can be likened to one huge (bio) chemical factory, and the diet provides the raw ingredients to enable the factory to produce the chemicals of life. A typical diet provides around 25 different foodstuffs per week, so try to expand the number of different foods in your diet to 40 or 50 per week to ensure you get all the raw ingredients for your personal chemical factory.

Dr Graham Matthews, Chiropractor

From Sprint to Ironman events, age need not be not a hurdle and you can still challenge yourself.

Triathlon's age group racing means you are never too old to compete and to race your peers.

Everyday Ironmen

Half and full-Ironman distance events are not all about elite athletes and dedicated training. People with real jobs, families and normal ability take on the challenge and succeed. Here are some tips and advice from experienced Ironmen.

must know

Ironman events started in the late 1970s as a challenge between fitness junkies. Today there are races all over the world, often filling up within hours or minutes of entries opening. You have to plan ahead and be ready with your credit card to just get to the start line!

Plan for the worst

Shift happens; that means getting kicked or punched in the swim, punctures, head winds, people drafting you, falling over, cramp, going off course, etc. Think 'what if...?' and plan for everything. If you expect the worst, anything less is a bonus!
Terry Harvey

Don't over-train

Exercise with others so long as it fits in with your training programme. Stretch yourself but be realistic with your goals – remember that a strong mind is just as important as a strong body, especially in long-distance events. Being healthy is not the same as being fit, so do what's necessary to stay healthy. At the end of the day, just enjoy your training and racing – stay focused but not obsessive and then you'll keep things in perspective.
Mike Gorman

Stay positive and focused

The training journey to Ironman is not always smooth, and you must remain positive and focused on the end result, even though periods of illness and injury may set you back occasionally. Ironman is a test of your mental strength and overcoming

everything that training and the race day throw at you, but the finish line is sure to bring a feeling of life-time achievement.
Kate O'Neil

Recovering as a vet

If you are a vet athlete, don't be afraid to have a complete rest and do no training at all for a good three or four days after a big event – our older bodies need longer to recover. We are only as good as the fuel we burn; poor nutrition equals poor recovery, so eat and drink smart.
John Milkins

Winter training

This is a great time to try out new drinks, gels and bars. Find out what agrees with you in the winter and then use it for all your training from spring and into the race season.
Brian Withers

Keep smiling

Race with a smile and thank the marshals – if it's not your job, you (and they) are doing it for the love of the sport, so enjoy it!
Peter Spencer

The bottom line is the finish line

All but a few hardy men and women should concern themselves with racing an Ironman. The idea is little more than this: you and a finish line. Do your best to get there, not someone else's. The bottom line is the finish line.
Chuckie V, Pro triathlete

Although the swim is only a small proportion of the event, you have to be out the water ready for a long day yet to be completed.

want to know more?

• There are Ironman races all over the world, often filling up within hours or minutes of entries opening. Plan ahead and be ready with your credit card to get to the start line. Look on:
www.ironman.com
www.xtri.com
www.ironmanlive.com
www.ironmanuk.com

11 Taking it further

When you can do a triathlon in your sleep, you may need to start looking for some bigger horizons to reach towards. It may be a faster time, a longer distance, an exciting location or outdoor freedom that you seek. When you are ready to challenge yourself, here are some ideas to get you thinking big.

Improving your PB

Focusing on a specific distance and not getting pulled into longer ones is a better mind set for some people. They like the sprint or Olympic distance, even the Super-Sprint distance, and want to get faster at their chosen distance and improve their PB.

Critical analysis

This is a stark look at how fast you did your triathlon and how much better you can realistically improve. It's not patting yourself on the back or being a day dreamer; this is logically breaking down how you performed and where it can get better. Extend this analysis to your training diary as well. Did you really do as much as you could have done or could you be more dedicated or better at time management? You cannot just try harder; you also will have to prepare even better if you want to improve your PB.

Seeking out one per cent

On a one-hour event, just improving by one per cent means you are 36 seconds faster. It may not seem like a lot but, with three sports, transitions and a lot of equipment to factor in, one per cent in five areas makes a significant difference. The hard work is making these theoretical one per cent changes happen. Never assume you are faster than what you have done. Being a hypothetical athlete who 'could have gone faster' will not do you any favours.

SWOT

By looking honestly at your strengths, weaknesses, opportunities and threats (SWOT) to performing better, you can find ways to help make you the faster triathlete you want to be. This does not mean you can always buy performance; the biggest gains come from the training, not the equipment.

Perhaps you could ask another triathlete to also rate your SWOT, and between you I am sure that you can identify some clear areas where you can improve.

Time trial testing

Once you have moved from completing to competing, you can use your training sessions to improve your fitness and test if you are getting faster. By setting up time trials in each sport once a month, you can assess if your training and equipment are leading to improved speed. Examples are swim 400–750m, bike 8–10 miles and run 3–5k. Expect to see your speed improving through February until the peak season.

Testing yourself against the clock in a one-sport event or your own home-grown courses is a great way to gauge progress and to achieve some top-end training.

Single-sport focus

You may be able to do all three sports back to back but single-sport focus can give you a new events calendar and allow an edge to be gained. Moving from a multisport to a one-sport athlete is not as dumb as it seems.

Short term

For many triathletes, focusing on one sport gets them away from doing all three sports to the same extent all the time. This may allow them to work on a swim weakness when the weather is too bad for much biking or when they are getting back to their preferred sport for a recharge. You do not have to be a three-sport expert all the time and taking some time out from each sport may even be a good thing to do occasionally. If it's planned and short term, it won't affect your long-term progress.

The positives and pitfalls

The up-side of single-sport focus is a hunger to get back to missed sports afterwards. Similarly, you get to really give a sport total focus. However, the downfall, especially in running, is that the overload can lead to injury. Cross training keeps you low on injury risk, but focusing on one sport can lead to muscle overload and injury.

Options

Swimming focus can include hitting the water every day for a week, an open-water event or entering a Masters' gala. On the bike again, you can get out every day and combine a time trial or harder group with your increased mileage to raise the overload level. Run training must be carefully increased, however, and it may be wise to include Aquajogging in the pool and soft surface running to reduce the chances of injury.

Be sure to build up slowly when you want to focus on one sport and tick over in the other two.

Duathlon

Duathlon, lacking the swim segment, is often seen by some people as the easier option to triathlon. However, with two runs to contest, it is actually harder than a triathlon. Use these events wisely and you can improve as a triathlete.

Season expanders

Duathlon is a way to include some tough workouts when triathlons are not available or convenient. Use them pre-season (March through April) to bring on your competition ability and test equipment. As triathlon winds down in late September, duathlons become abundant, so you can extend the season for several weeks by incorporating run-bike-run events. Draw a clear line when the season ends, as you must have your required post-season recuperation period followed by winter base building.

Form testers

Many short duathlons are organized by tri clubs to give members a chance to compete when or where swim facilities are not convenient. These can be integrated into mid-week or weekends as quality workouts to see how well you are doing. The key with duathlon racing is simple: treat the first run like a cruise, then get on the bike and start to race proper. That way, you run off the bike strong, like a triathlon feels.

Powerman

As the ultimate duathlon challenge, the Powerman series (www.powerman.org) combines events all

over the world in a series of races over varying distances. The long-distance version (Zofingen) consists of a gruelling 10k–150k–30k challenge, and it is considered the Ironman version of duathlon. Specialist duathletes, focusing on this two-sport event, compete in different age groups right up to professional level. It is a sport in its own right which some people prefer to triathlon.

Duathlon also requires focus on three disciplines: pacing the first run; strong biking; and a second run off the bike. You need to be quick with your shoe transitions.

The next challenge

From a local pool-based sprint triathlon or short do-a-duathlon, many people find that going abroad to an international event or ultra-long distance is their next challenge. For those triathletes who want to travel and compete, there are many opportunities.

Opportunities and commitment

Triathlon is an international sport that has grown up with travel as part of the ethos of competing. There are hundreds of events held in the UK, but by travelling you can experience racing in some of the world's most beautiful and challenging environments. From Ironman events held in super-hot Lanzarote or Hawaii to highly competitive age group racing at the annual Age Group World Championships over Sprint, Olympic, Middle and Long course distances, thre is something for everyone. There is also the emergence of the 70.3 Half Ironman (1.9, 90, 21k) distance as well as the Double-Olympic format (3, 80, 20k).

Time and budget

These races require a significant financial outlay, time to travel and additional expenses, such as accommodation, race entry fees and travelling costs. An international event can be linked into a holiday or used as a lifetime experience to race one of the really big events of the triathlon calendar. Most triathletes usually move on to these new challenges after two or three years of competing in smaller events; building up their experience before competing gives a logic to the process.

The four rules

As we have already seen in this book, triathlon is the perfect combination of fun, fitness and achievement. It serves to help athletes learn and be motivated as well as inspiring those around them. However, bear the following four rules in mind when you trek through your triathlon adventures.

Rule one – do no harm

You must not knowingly harm your body through excess; it can do wonderful things if you nurture it and feed it well, so look after it.

Rule two – balance the books

You must always ensure that you recognize those people who help you and that you try to pay them back in some way for what they give you.

Rule three – lead by example

At all times, try to be a good role model for the sport. Play by the rules, and be a positive advert for the triathlon lifestyle, helping and motivating others to achieve their goals.

Rule four – give something back

It takes many people many hours with much sweat and toil to put on triathlon events and races and keep clubs together. Be aware of this and give something back to the sport you love by being sure to add your sweat to volunteering, sponsoring or even organizing an event near you.

want to know more?

• To find out more about staying fit and healthy, and getting the balance between life and sport right, read the following:
Body, Mind and Sport, Douillard (Three Rivers Press)
In Fitness and in Health, Maffetone (David Barmore Prouctions)
Mental Training for Peak Performance, Ungerleider (Rodale)
The Te of Piglet, Hoff (Methuen)

Glossary

Aero: Any bike part shaped to improve a rider's speed by reducing air turbulence.

Aerobic: Exercise at low to moderate intensity using a mixture of fat and carbohydrates.

Anaerobic: Exercise at high intensity using carbohydrate exclusively.

AquaJogging: Running with a flotation device around the waist as a non-impact alternative to tarmac or trails.

Bands: Stretchy rubber strips designed to be used as resistance work or pre-swim warm up.

Bilateral: Breathing to both sides whilst swimming, usually alternating every third stroke.

Bottom bracket: Central axis the bicycle cranks rotate on.

Brick: A cycle session followed by a running session; may be made into multiple efforts, e.g. bike-run-bike-run.

Cadence: Number of revolutions per minute of the bicycle cranks.

Carbo-loading: Increase in carbohydrate-rich foods, e.g. pasta, rice, bread, breakfast cereals and potatoes, in the last three or four days before a race.

Cassette: Cluster of 5-10 sprockets fixed to the centre of the rear wheel, allowing gears to be selected using the handlebar-mounted shifting system.

Catch: Stage of the swim stroke after full extension when the hand begins to apply backward pressure on the water whilst the elbow remains high.

Chainring: Round rings connected to the cranks, typically with tooth counts of 39 (hills) and 53 (flats).

Chainset: Lever connecting the bottom bracket to the bike pedals, typically 165-175mm long (also known as cranks).

Chaingang: A group ride at moderate to high effort, each rider taking time to work at the front of the group, then recover at the back.

Cool down: A 5-10 minute period at the end of training sessions to allow heat to be dissipated, muscles lightly stretched and the triathlete to acquire a relaxed mindset.

Dehydration: Drop in body fluids that, if significant (more than two per cent of body weight) can result in reduced performance and serious health implications if fluids are not taken and exercise ceased.

Drafting: Riding close behind another rider in order to reduce effort by 20-40 per cent; if you are closer than five metres in a race you are deemed to be cheating and you may be penalized or disqualified.

Electrolyte drink: Fluid with added electrolyte salts, such as sodium or potassium, to aid fluid replacement during and after exercise.

Fins: Large rubber paddle-shaped accessories that fit on the feet for easy progress through the water; ideal for some drills.

Gel: Carbohydrate energy product with syrup-like consistency, so that fuel can be taken in without any chewing or much digestion.

Glycogen: Carbohydrate stored with water inside the muscle. Glycogen can be used as a fuel to provide muscle movement.

Hand paddles: Flat or curved plastic board worn on the hand, so a greater force can be applied to the water.

Heart rate (HR): Number of beats per minute of your heart muscle.

Heart Rate Monitor: Device using a chest strap to sense the HR and display it as a beats-per-minute number.

Hypoxic: Training with less breaths taken per minute than is comfortable or normal.

Intervals: Periods of increased effort that are grouped in blocks within a session, e.g. 4 x 3-minute intervals with 2 minutes light exercise between each.

Kick board: Foam float held ahead of the swimmer to focus on front, back and on-the-side kicking drills.

Lactate: By-product of working at high-intensity that increases to a point where you must slow down and it is recycled and used as a fuel for working muscles (also known as lactic acid).

Maximum Heart Rate: The HR (heart rate) that is recorded at the hardest effort that you can give (also known as HRmax).

Open water: Swims in lakes, rivers and the sea, which normally require you to wear a wetsuit.

Perceived exertion: Your perception of how hard you are trying: may be a term such as 'easy' or 'hard', or a number, e.g. 8 on a scale of 10.

Personal Best (PB): Your fastest ever time for a particular distance – it may be in swim, bike, run or multisport events.

Pull buoy: Foam float that fits between the legs to lift the hips when swimming (less useful than fins).

Pull/Press: Middle phases of the swim stroke where the hand is pulled under the body and pressed backwards to alongside the outer thigh.

Quick release (QR): Press-shut lever that allows bike wheels to be easily removed and replaced for travel or repairs.

Race belt: Elastic waist band holding the race number, saving holes in trisuits and easing transitions.

Glossary

Recovery: Act of lifting the arm from next to the thigh, forwards, with a high elbow until the hand drops in front of the shoulder to enter the water.

Rest Interval (RI): Time between intervals or drills in which you recover and focus on the next effort and good form.

Sculling: Using the hands to create lift by subtle deflections of the hand and wrist angle.

Speed-distance monitor: Used in bike or run sessions to calculate the distance travelled and current speed.

Split: A time for each segment of a race, e.g. swim split or bike split.

Stroke count: Number of strokes taken to travel the length of either a 25m or 50m pool.

T1: First transition which begins at the end of the swim and stops as the rider mounts the bike.

T2: Second transition which begins as the rider dismounts the bike and ends as the runner leaves the transition area.

Taper: Reduced quantity of training, including higher intensity efforts, preceding an event.

Time trial (TT): Race against the clock over a known distance, e.g. 500m swim or 10-mile bike.

Transition: Fenced area in which bikes are stored with other items, e.g. run shoes or race belt.

Tri bars: Two padded cups with forward pointing extensions for riding more comfortably faster (also known as aerobars).

Tri suit: One- or two-piece tri-specific clothing that removes need to change from swim, to bike to run, saving time.

Turbo Trainer: Slang for an indoor trainer; a device that holds a bicycle in place, applying resistance to the rear wheel, avoiding road cycling in bad weather or poor light.

Warm up: A 5–10 minute gradual increase in pace that starts each training session to prepare the mind and body for harder work.

Wetsuit : One- or two-piece neoprene suit that retains heat and increases flotation; only used in open water events.

Need to know more?

Governing bodies

British Triathlon Federation
PO Box 25, Loughborough LE11 3WX
tel: 01509 226161
fax: 01509 226165
www.britishtriathlon.org
email: info@britishtriathlon.org

Amateur Swimming Association (ASA)
Harold Fern House, Derby Square,
Loughborough,
Leicestershire LE11 5AL
tel: 01509 618 700
fax: 01509 618 701
www.britishswimming.org
email: customerservices@swimming.org

British Cycling
National Cycling Centre, Stuart Street,
Manchester M11 4DQ
tel: 870 871 2000
www.britishcycling.org.uk
email: info@britishcycling.org.uk

UK Athletics
Athletics House, Central Boulevard,
Blythe Valley Park, Solihull
West Midlands B90 8AJ
tel: 0870 998 6800
www.ukathletics.net

Internet resources

Training camps, travel, events

209 Events
Running camps, events and holidays
www.209events.com

Sports Tours International
Training camps for triathlon
www.sportstoursinternational.co.uk

Club La Santa
Sports and active holiday resort in the
Canary Islands
www.clublasanta.com

Ironman UK
Half and Full Ironman race organizers
www.ironmanuk.com

Trail Plus
Running and adventure events
www.trailplus.com

American Bicycle Group
www.americanbicyclegroup.com

DBmax
Triathlon, Rowathon and Duathlon
www.dbmax.co.uk

Need to know more?

TriFerris Promotions
Duathlon, triathlon and off-road events
www.triferris.com

Runners World
Race listings and running advice
www.runnersworld.co.uk

Peak Performance
Sports science articles and information
www.pponline.co.uk

Trainsmart
Online training diary and guidance
www.trainsmart.com

Otag Technologies
Training diary software
www.ismarttrain.com

Joe Beer
Author's own website with information
on multi-sports coaching
www.JBST.com

Magazines

220 Triathlon
UK's only monthly triathlon magazine
www.220magazine.com

Cycling Plus
All aspects of cycling and cycle news
www.cyclingplus.co.uk

Podcasts

Training for Triathlon
Regular podcast on all things multisport
http://tinyurl.com/y3482m

Podrunner
Free workout music mixes for training to
www.djsteveboy.com/podrunner.html

Author's acknowledgements

Thanks to the following companies and individuals for their support in making this book possible: adidas, Polar Electro and Bottlestore; Mark Sinclair (adidas), Chris Hewings (American Bicycle Group), Stuart Hayes (adidas), Anne Kaarlela (Polar), Marc Honold (PowerBar Europe), SouthFork and Club La Santa; Hampton Pool for their help and use of facilities; the organizers & athletes Langport Triathlon; Rob Bell, Marzena Bogdanowicz, Paul Chambers, Mark Lees, Jason Maddocks, Louise McKee, Toby Radcliffe, Alan Ward and Suzanne White; Sam, Heather and Rolando for their immense patience; and all the athletes over the years who have put their trust in me and amazed me with their performances; my Mum and Dad for supporting me as I studied and giving me a chance they never had; my son Seth for putting all this into perspective and my soul mate and wife Sharon for her never-ending ability to put up with me and show me the way in life.

Index

⟡ Collins need to know?

Look out for these recent titles in Collins' practical and accessible need to know? series.

Other titles in t

se
hone
ting

ation
oks,

k